# Understanding
# Industry Today

G. M. J. Richardson

Edited by A. S. Wood

David & Charles
Newton Abbot   London   North Pomfret (Vt)

This book is the result of a series of booklets which were prepared to support the Understanding Industry programme devised by Gerry Richardson. The material was written and prepared by practising managers specialising in the subjects which form the chapter headings of this edition.

Understanding Industry is managed by
and funded through
The Understanding Industry Trust (UIT)
91 Waterloo Road
London SE1 8XP
Registered Charity No 202 808 822

**British Library Cataloguing in Publication Data**

Richardson, G.M.J.
    Understanding industry today.
    1. Great Britain—Industries
    I. Title      II. Wood, Antony
    338.0941      HC256 6

    ISBN 0-7153-8951 3

© Industrial Training Foundation 1984, Understanding Industry Trust 1986
First Edition 1984
Second revised edition 1986

Typeset by ABM Typographics Limited Hull
and printed in Great Britain
by Redwood Burn Ltd Trowbridge Wilts
for David & Charles Publishers plc
Brunel House   Newton Abbot   Devon

Published in the United States of America
by David & Charles Inc
North Pomfret   Vermont 05053   USA

# CONTENTS

# FOREWORD TO THE SECOND EDITION

This book is called 'Understanding Industry Today' so we need to keep it as up-to-date as possible. Our industries are changing fast and many of them are world leaders in their field. If we are to reflect these standards and the extent of technological change the text must be revised every year or so. This new edition contains some important improvements:

1  The first chapter has been altered to put greater emphasis on those who support wealth creation.
2  All businesses start with a good idea. Commercial ideas in particular must aim to meet the needs of customers. This is the function of the Marketing department and consequently we have put the chapter on Marketing immediately after the Introduction.

The biggest single change is the inclusion of a new chapter (Chapter 8) to introduce the idea of small businesses and to confirm how important they are. Small businesses are very flexible and in an age of change flexibility is probably the key quality.

If you feel that one day you would like to run your own business you should read this final chapter. Also if you are still in education, see if your school or college will run an Understanding Industry (UI) course. Ideally this will be followed by the formation of a Young Enterprise (YE) company. During Industry Year UI and YE got together in order to offer students a joint package. The UI course offers the theory of business in an enjoyable and realistic way and this theory can then be put into practice by running your own YE company. Last year over 17,000 young achievers handled real money and real problems and if you would like to know more the address of Young Enterprise can be found on page 134.

Understanding Industry Today now tells you what you can expect to find in a modern British company—be it large or small. I hope you enjoy the new sections and that the whole book portrays something of the fascination and excitement of what it means to be in business, and especially industry.

Lord Caldecote

# ACKNOWLEDGEMENTS

It would not be possible to create a book such as this without reference to much of the best in modern British industry.

We are indebted to a large number of people but would particularly like to thank the following for their interest and support. Without such help this book would not have been possible.

G. E. A. Barker, Anne Bilsland, R. C. B. Drew, Maurice Lainchbury, R. G. Moore, John Ryle and Alan Thompson—all from 3i Consultants—Michael Brewer of PERA and also K. A. White and M. E. Robinson. The section on retailing in Chapter 2 was provided by Ray Rowsell and Mr E. F. T. Cribb of Freemans plc; whilst John Sheppards of the Association of Scientific Technical and Managerial Staff contributed to the preparation of Chapter 6. Many of the statistics were checked by Louise Amor of the 3i library, Solihull, to whom we are particularly grateful. Much useful comment was received from the trustees of the Understanding Industry Trust (UIT)—Kenneth Adams, Dr. D. V. Atterton, N. P. Bailey, R. C. R. Blackledge, Viscount Caldecote, Sir Monty Finniston, The Lady Howe, Sir Anthony Jolliffe, I. N. Momtchiloff and Jeremy Leigh Pemberton.

Expert advice was provided by members of the specialist engineering institutions including: The Institution of Mechanical and General Technician Engineers, Dr Elizabeth Laverick of the Institution of Electrical Engineers and J. A. Napper of the Institution of Production Engineers.

Special thanks are due to Dr Eric Bates and his team at the Industry Education Unit of the Department of Trade and Industry for their continued support and also to David Dyer, Director of the A Level Business Studies project, for his help with the revision of Chapter 1.

This revised and fully updated edition contains a new section on the importance of small businesses. This was written by Cliff Johnson of the Durham University Business School with support from Cim Mellor of Business in the Community. Without the help of these contributors the book would lack an essential element of the modern business scene.

Antony Wood
(Editor)

# 1
# INTRODUCTION (INDUSTRY AND COMMERCE IN SOCIETY)

## Outline

Industry is about people and their work.

In this book the word 'industry' is used as a shorthand term to describe the making and selling of goods as well as services. However, it will be useful at the outset to be clear about the basic difference between manufacturing industry and the service industries. A manufacturing operation is one which takes raw materials in on one side and converts them, through the use of machinery, into 'finished goods' on the other. Industry always involves a conversion process and the use of machinery. Examples might be tinplate into food cans, plastic resin into children's toys, and wood into chairs. Marks & Spencer is not a manufacturer because it does not make anything. In common with other service industries, such as banking, insurance, hotels and leisure, transport, hairdressing etc, it does not provide finished goods. What it does do is to distribute and market the articles made by British industry (over 90 per cent of M & S goods are made in the UK), and thereby provides a service which people need.

The business of making and selling goods and services in a modern society is complex. Nonetheless because it is *people* who do the making and selling (and the buying!) the commercial world is more about people than anything else. However many machines are used and however much we hear about the power of computers, it is *people* who control their operation.

The essence of any industrial or business enterprise is successful co-operation between people. Each individual uses his or her personal skills—some manual, some mental—and does so as part of a team. In each organisation some will do, some will direct, but all are part of the same team.

People have always had to work for a living, first as hunter-gatherers, then as subsistence farmers, now as members of an industrial society. Working for personal survival and for the comfort of one's family is and always has been a fundamental part of living. The fulfilment of this deep-seated habit and drive brings a satisfying sense of purpose to people's lives; productive work itself can be valued as highly as the end result—as with the gardener whose joy is in growing things but not necessarily in selling them.

From earliest times the importance of work has been impressed on us. In order to ensure survival, the idea of a work ethic or the innate 'goodness' of toil has developed. Today that ethic is being challenged: 'work' has been made more efficient, and conditions of employment are steadily improving. These developments are being brought about largely by the advent of new technology and they mean that, whilst we can look forward to more leisure time, we also have to face high unemployment levels and uncertainty. These trends will continue—especially as the microchip frees us from the more mundane but labour-intensive tasks.

Faced with these changes it is tempting to believe that manufacturing is not important. This feeling is, to some extent, reinforced by our remoteness from the production process. Nowadays it is not possible to be personally involved with the creation of the goods we both need and enjoy. The ordinary packet of fish fingers is simply found on the supermarket shelf. In fact its arrival there has involved hundreds of people and many decisions—right through from the trawler captain's plan to fish the North Sea, the manufacture of the product in Norway, distribution, packaging design and so on. Every product has a story to tell but because it is easy to take the articles all around us for granted (and because most of us know so little about the manufacturing sector) it is tempting to think industry no longer matters. But it does.

It matters at a personal level because we need the goods that industry produces—without them we would be naked in a field. It matters at a social level because we cannot improve our lot without the tools to do so. Writing on this theme a hundred years ago John Ruskin said, 'Observe the merchant's [or manufacturer's] function . . . is to provide for the nation. Five great intellectual professions, relating to daily necessities of life, have hitherto existed—the soldier, the pastor, the physician, the lawyer and the merchant.' The key point here is that the doctor cannot heal without the bandages, hypodermics, hospital beds etc that industry provides. And the point applies to all the other activities which make up our way of life.

But industry is also important at a national level. The UK's share of world trade in manufactured goods has fallen from 26 per cent in 1950 to an estimated 7.9 per cent in 1983. Similarly in 1983, for the first time since records were kept, the UK became a net importer of manufactured products. This affects everyone in society for two reasons. First, because we are a trading nation and, at the simplest level, need to sell goods in order to buy the 40 per cent of food we do not grow ourselves. Secondly, because the government relies on the wealth-creating sector (agriculture, manufacturing and the service industries) to provide the money to pay for hospitals, defence, the care of the elderly, education, the police, unemployment benefit and so on. In the financial year 1986/7 the government needs to raise £138.4 billion from taxes in order to pay for the services our advanced Western society expects. If industry is not able to supply its quota of wealth then the quality of national life must decline.

Thus it is clear that industry is a major contributor to society because it provides:

1 Goods and services.
2 Incomes and jobs.
3 Revenue for taxes.
4 Products for export.
5 Money for future investment.

As we move forward change will be the order of the day. It is likely that the service sector of the economy will expand, and as old industries decline, new ones will take their place.

This book does not set out to offer solutions to the problems these changes will pose. Its aim is to explain the way in which industry is organised and to examine its chief functions. These functions have to interact and by doing so allow industry to perform its purpose. What that purpose is we shall examine shortly. Armed with more facts the student will be better able to understand the complexity of the industrial base; to explore the possibilities for the future and to focus on the challenge before us.

INDUSTRY IN SOCIETY

As mentioned earlier, industry provides all the goods and services that we need. Almost everything that we see around us has been produced by industry—even much of our food. We cannot escape from it, and therein lies its importance to us.

Industry reacts to our changing needs and adapts itself to meet them. Chipboard has been developed as a result of people's reluctance to pay for solid wood furniture, their concern for the preservation of natural resources, and the damage caused by central heating.

Sometimes industry is instrumental in stimulating change. This is usually because the development of new techniques, materials and designs offers previously unsuspected advantages. People did not know they wanted chipboard furniture until it was found to be cheaper than wood and to cope with the ravages of dry atmosphere.

Sometimes industry has changes forced upon it, either as a result of competition or because customers are not satisfied with what they are getting. However, industry cannot impose new products on society if there is no recognition of their worth. Many clever inventions fail commercially for the simple reason that they are not needed.

In providing goods and services to meet our needs industry gives work to millions of people and helps to create our wealth; products are brought into existence and money is earned to purchase the things we need or want, both personally and as a society.

## The Creation of Wealth

WHAT IS WEALTH?

Everyone has their own idea of the meaning of the word 'wealth'. Frequently it is related to individuals and in this sense wealth comes to have a quantitive meaning: a 'wealthy' person is one who appears to have money and a rich assortment of expensive belongings. In fact any material possessions are wealth. Thus the wealth of the nation is the sum total of all the goods and materials that we possess collectively (eg roads, clean water) or as individuals (eg homes, stereos). Our coal and oil deposits, and the nation's work-force, with its many individual skills, are all part of the country's wealth. To enable us to continue these thoughts we need to define what is meant by wealth.

MONEY

This is a convenient means of measuring and exchanging wealth. Its function in society is to act as a lubricant, enabling us to deal with our wealth, but it is not wealth itself.

INCOME

Usually, but not always, this is measured in money terms and can be defined as the extent to which we are able to command wealth in a particular period. It is earned by the contribution we make to wealth creation or it is given to us at times in our life when we are "dependant". Obvious examples of those who are dependant are the very young, the unemployed, the retired.

This diagram does not tell the whole story. Increasingly some housewives are doing part-time work and are therefore moving between box B and box A shown above. **However in this chapter we are concerned solely with those operating in box A – the wealth creators. For them to operate effectively they need the continued backing of those in the support services (box B).**

The latest figures show that in 1984 we created £242 billion as a result of all the work that went on in the country. This is known as the GDP or Gross Domestic Product and can be added to the other assets, such as buildings, machinery etc, that we already have.

### WHY WEALTH?

Other nations may be more or less fortunate than we are. Just as the developing countries cannot provide themselves with all the amenities of the twentieth century at a stroke, we cannot maintain— let alone improve—our standards without the wealth to pay for our aspirations.

It must be stressed that this fact applies equally to the capitalist society of the West and to the directed economies of the Soviet and Eastern blocks. However it is expressed, distributed and used the creation of wealth is the basis of any standard of living.

### WEALTH CREATION

In the modern world people are often far removed from the things which their work helps to make—unlike a carpenter at the workbench. When we buy, say, a cassette player, we usually don't know the people who made it. We are not aware of the way it was produced and the commercial factors which led to its particular design.

Some of the products of industry are trivial, inessential or even harmful. Also it is true that some jobs in industry are unpleasant, and it is difficult to devise ways of improving the lot of people who do them. Yet for the most part industry and commerce provide an enormous variety of goods and services which enrich our lives, as well as a multitude of jobs to challenge and satisfy our creative needs.

A simple example of wealth creation is a carpenter converting relatively inexpensive material into furniture. The difference between the cost of the wood and the price of the finished article is the wealth which has been created. It is the value which the customer places on the skill used. It is not all profit for the carpenter: much of the added value will pay for the general 'overheads' of the business, such as rent and heating plus the wages of any helpers.

The more elaborate the article, or the more effort and time put into the quality of its finish, the greater the value added. Wealth is created by adding value to raw materials, but this need not be a physical activity. It is important to understand that the service industries like banking, transport and entertainment can also create wealth. Their raw materials and work tend to be intangible, but are

Figure 1

nonetheless real.

Some figures may be helpful in assessing the value of industry to our society (see Figure 2). Note that only about half the total population of the country are paid for what they do; the rest includes the elderly, the sick, children and young people in education, those who cannot find work, and those whose job is to stay at home and look after their families. Of the 24.3 million who have jobs less than a quarter are in manufacturing industry; about a fifth are in jobs which

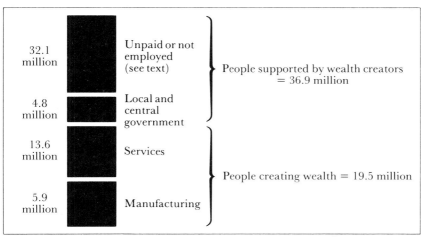

Total population = 56.4 million
Source: CSO

Figure 2

support wealth creation (civil administration, education, the health service etc) and the remainder work in the service industries. As is typical for most advanced economies more people are engaged in service industries than in manufacturing. However, the most important fact is that out of a total population of 56 million less than half are the wealth creators. The rest of the people are wealth consumers.

It is important to understand the implications of this fact. To put it another way it means that out of every hundred people in the country thirty-five are charged with producing the wealth the other sixty-five cannot create for themselves. As the population ages and society changes economists expect this ratio to alter and move towards a ratio of 75:25 by the end of this decade.

This is not to deny the interdependence of those who create wealth with the rest of the community. Industry needs the infrastructure of government and the security of an efficient police force; we all need doctors, teachers and social workers irrespective of their role in the wealth-creating game. Without such an infrastructure industry could not do its job and one of the main purposes of wealth creation is to make these civilising benefits available. This point is not at issue. What must be understood is that a country can only have these things if it understands how they are funded and can create the necessary monies.

THE CIRCULATION AND DISTRIBUTION OF WEALTH

What happens to all the wealth that is created? Wealth is distributed by using money. A large proportion is paid to the work-force as wages, and much of it passes to other companies for the purchase of machinery, vehicles, stationery etc. (See Chapter 3 and the money-go-round.) People often spend their wages locally on the purchase of goods and services for the home, thus keeping the money circulating in their own district.

Quite a lot goes to the Government (£138.4 billion in 1986/87) in the form of taxes to pay for all the artistic, humanitarian and non-commercial aspects of our community. Hospitals, schools, museums, pensions and the many welfare functions we have come to expect are all supported from the wealth created by the businesses of the nation and the people who work in them.

In our society the role of government is a dominant one. Taxation is raised on the profit of companies (called corporation tax), the income of individuals, and from various duties and indirect taxes—

## Central and local government spending

1986–7                    £ billion

| | |
|---|---|
| Planned spending on goods and services (including wages and salaries of government employees) | |
| Defence | 18.5 |
| Subsidies to regions | 14.8 |
| National Health Service | 17.7 |
| Education | 14.3 |
| Overseas Aid | 2.0 |
| Agriculture, fisheries and food | 2.2 |
| Industry, energy, trade and employment | 5.4 |
| Arts | 0.7 |
| Transport | 4.8 |
| Housing | 2.8 |
| Environment | 3.6 |
| Law and Order | 5.5 |
| Social Security | 42.8 |
| Others | 3.6 |
| Reserve etc | 4.5 |
| | 143.2 |

Note: £4.8 billion due from privitisation should be deducted from the above figure to give a total expenditure of £138.4 billion.

Source: The Government's Expenditure Plans 1986–7 (Cmnd 9702–1)

Figure 3

such as VAT. The revenue thus raised, as we have said, is used in many ways for the benefit of us all through the provision of education, the health service, social security and so on. Government spending also helps the circulation of wealth (as does personal spending) and much of the money collected in taxes returns to industry in the form of government or local authority contracts, or the purchase of goods and services. The way our collective wealth is distributed is a matter of political policy. Governments decide what services should be provided by the state, at what level of expenditure, and how the taxation system should be organised in order to collect sufficient money.

The most important point is that government cannot itself create wealth. It cannot print money. It can only redistribute what has already been created.

IMPORTS AND EXPORTS

It is not possible for Great Britain to stand alone, creating and distributing its wealth in a vacuum. Most of our raw materials have to be imported and have to be paid for. Although currency is used as the vehicle for settling international trading accounts, the underlying bargain is a swop—we buy iron ore and sell machinery.

Just as with government spending we cannot invent money to pay for imports. Third world countries (such as South Korea and Taiwan) are now developing their own industry, and competing in areas which were once our preserve.

However, despite the loss mentioned earlier of our share of world trade, Britain is still one of the world's major exporting countries. The current trading account for 1985 was in surplus and during the year the country exported manufactured goods to the value of £78.4 billion. Every month between £5 and £8 billion worth of manufactured goods are sold abroad. The problem is, of course, that we should aim to sell more—to pay for the food we need; to pay for all our imports and to pay for the things we expect in a civilised society.

In order to do this, and to cope with a trend of increasing competition from the rest of the world, we must deploy all our resources; increase our efficiency; develop new markets and produce new products with high added value.

ADDED VALUE

The concept of added value needs some explanation. The generally accepted definition is that it is the difference between what a company pays for all the bought-in goods and services it needs and the money it generates from sales. Put at its simplest it represents the conversion process that we discussed on page 13. The cost of 'goods and services' will include such items as raw materials, rent, rates, electricity and telephone charges. The goods must then be sold and the difference between the sale price and the above costs can be thought of as the value the people working to produce them have added by their skill.

Those outside industry sometimes think that what is now left is available for free spending, but this is not so. The remainder of the added value has to go to:

1 The employees to pay for their wages, national insurance and pensions.
2 The shareholders (who have invested their savings or funds in the company)—to provide for interest and dividends.
3 Suppliers—to pay for new machinery, buildings etc.
4 The government—to meet tax demands and help fund the public purse.

What is left after this is the profit or operating surplus.

PROFIT

We have already encountered the word 'profit' in looking at the value that the carpenter added by turning wood into furniture and in discussing the concept of added value. More will be said on the subject in the chapter on Finance.

It is easy to think of profit only in the context of monetary gain, but we might consider that the profit society obtains from industry has a more general meaning. Everyone stands to gain if an enterprise is successful. The employees enjoy improved job security, better wages and conditions; customers can reasonably expect reliable delivery dates and decent quality; suppliers are more likely to receive regular orders and better prices and socially desirable activities (such as reducing pollution) become easier to fund. In addition more profit means that more tax is paid (to the benefit of the community) and shareholders can receive a higher return on their investment.

We all profit from profitable industry.

## The Key Aspects of Industry

The purpose of any business enterprise is to provide the goods and services which people require and to do so at a profit. In fact the task of trying to define the true purpose of commercial organisations has long been, and will continue to be, a subject of debate. You may well have your own view. What is certain is that a business cannot stay alive long enough to achieve its purposes unless it makes money. Survival therefore is a crucial element of the business environment.

We have already discussed the difference between industry and commerce and some economists would wish to differentiate further by talking of other categories, such as 'primary', 'secondary' and 'tertiary' industries.

However they are described, all businesses need certain basic functions and it is these—namely, finance, marketing, technical development, production, personnel and management—that form the core of this book. We have sought to explain these functions regardless of the size of the operation, and the book covers many aspects of commerce as well.

A company can succeed when the interrelationships between its different functions are in balance—when the team is working together well. No one function ranks above the others, although the emphasis given to each will vary from one company to another. Here they have been described not in order of importance but in a sequence which will be logical to the student.

## FINANCE—THE BUSINESS OF MONEY

Industry needs money for the purchase of factories, machines, raw materials, services and labour. The needs of commerce are similar but do not really involve the purchase of machines and raw materials. Every operation needs to get money from somewhere, both to get the business going and to provide enough cash to keep it alive. Finance for these requirements can come from shareholders and loans from banks or financial institutions. Much of the cash needed will come from regular trading income and profits.

Profit in this sense means the gains made by selling at a higher price than buying, not the overall profit that a successful undertaking might hope to achieve for the benefit of its owners. The meaning of the word 'profit' will be discussed further at several points in the book.

## MARKETING

Business enterprise exist by selling their goods. Chapter 2 deals with the way in which markets are found; how products are designed to meet carefully measured demands; how pricing affects profitability and how customers are encouraged to buy goods. It is a key function because, 'There is only one valid definition of business purpose—to create a customer' (Peter Drucker).

## DESIGN AND DEVELOPMENT

Modern industry is increasingly based on technology and not on craftsmanship. The technical activities of industry are mostly concerned with developing new products (including research into new materials) and improvements to the existing product range—including quality, cost, performance and efficient production. All this is covered in Chapter 4 but other aspects of technology will be considered throughout the book.

Scientific advance has brought about great improvements in our ability to handle data. The computer is not limited to any one sphere or function in business and can be found everywhere. Routine administration is an ideal task for the computer but it can also handle the huge amount of information needed for complicated business decisions. Some of the applications of computers will be covered in the chapters on design and development, production, and management.

MANUFACTURING AND PRODUCTION

Industry is about making things and production is at the heart of this process. The manufacturing function is unique to industry and the presence of machines turning raw materials into finished (or part-finished) goods is the key difference between industry and commerce.

The organisation of a manufacturing activity is complex. The rate, quality and quantity of work must be controlled accurately to avoid waste and meet demand. Production engineers are among the most highly skilled people in the community and their role and some of the day-to-day problems they face are looked at in Chapter 5.

PEOPLE

The importance of people in organisations has already been explained. Helping people to work together is often thought of as the responsibility of the personnel department but in fact it involves everyone in the enterprise, especially managers and supervisors.

The role of the trade union movement, the legal implications of employment, pay, and the motivation of people are all covered in Chapter 6, together with other aspects of human relations.

MANAGEMENT

The proper co-ordination of all the resources available—human and material—is the key to the success of any business enterprise. This is the job of management. The qualities which good managers need and the process of decision-making which is their stock-in-trade are discussed in Chapter 7.

The special role of the directors of a company is covered on page 25. In considering their contribution it must not be forgotten that they too are managers and workers.

## The Structure of a Business

A business can be organised in many different ways: there are as many solutions to the organisational problem as there are busi- nesses! However, they all have to have a legal framework from which to operate and the most common types of operation are the sole trader, the partnership and the limited company (abbreviated to PLC or plc see page 49). Within these legal groupings commercial organisations range from those with only two people to those like ICI which has about 115,000 employees in the UK and world-wide.

Let's suppose that you want to start a business. How easy is it?

### Sole traders

The simplest form of enterprise is when one individual sets up an independent business. You are then known as a *sole trader* and may or may not employ other people. You put up the money to start the job in hand and any debts are your own; if the business fails you will incur the penalties of bankruptcy with the consequent risk of hardship.

No special permission is needed to become a sole trader, but in view of the risks involved it would be wise to plan the business carefully before spending money on stock or renting premises.

### Partnerships

If several people want to trade, then it may be best to form a *partnership*. A partnership is two or more people who undertake a joint venture for profit. In order to safeguard the members of the partnership an *agreement* is needed. It sets out the extent of each partner's interest in the business, and their liability for it. In many respects a partnership operates like a sole trader but the chief difference is that the partners will share the risks and the rewards. However, each is still personally liable in the event of failure.

Most small shopkeepers and many professional people like architects are sole traders; the most common partnerships are those formed by solicitors and accountants.

### Limited companies

These are organisations to which individuals have subscribed share capital, ie put up some of their own money. Their personal responsibility for debts is 'limited' to the size of their shareholding or stake in the company. Providing there are at least two of you anybody can start a limited company and in most circumstances it makes sense to do so because it gives a large measure of security to the shareholders and their families.

A company is a legal entity and is distinct from the persons (shareholders) who own it. It can sue and be sued and, by inference, accept and discharge responsibilities. If the owners are not responsible for the company's debts beyond their shareholding it follows that one of their responsibilities is to trade within its credit capacity. If its debts exceed its assets (ie its ability to pay) it becomes insolvent and any further trading is a criminal offence. While the shareholders are in some measure protected from the risk of personal bankruptcy, the officers of the company become criminally liable if they knowingly continue to trade when the company is insolvent. In this way the public is protected from the 'limit' on the owners' liability.

Various Companies Acts have been enacted over the years and their provisions have now been consolidated into the Companies Act 1985. They set out the rules for the constitution, management and dissolution of companies in Britain.

A company must be registered at Companies' House (which is now in Cardiff ) or Exchequer Chambers in Edinburgh. If you set up your own company it will require both a *memorandum of association*, setting out the name, location, proposed activities etc, and *articles of association* which are the regulations agreed by the shareholders.

The registration fee for a new company is only £50. A new company can be based on the existing business of a sole trader or it might be an entirely new venture. At the end of 1985 there were 853,791 companies in Great Britain, split between 850,326 private and 3,465 public (source: Companies House).

PUBLIC AND PRIVATE COMPANIES

A private company cannot offer shares to, or raise money from the public. Shares however can and do change hands. A private company no longer has to restrict the transferability of its shares although it may do so by making provision in the company's Articles of Association in order to retain the 'family' nature of the company. For example, a sole trader might wish to form a limited company because the enterprise has become too large and he or she may not wish to bear all the financial responsibility alone. They may not, however, wish to lose control of the venture and may want to keep the reward for all their work within the family. The answer is to form a (private) limited company with provision in its Articles restricting the transferability of its shares (see page 49).

In November 1980 The Stock Exchange created the Unlisted Securities Market and made it possible for businesses with less than £5 million worth of capital to issue shares and go public. Since that time 411 small companies have joined the USM and it has been a great success. The cost of issuing shares is kept to a minimum and companies like Merrydown Wine, FKB and Pineapple Studios have been able to raise the additional funds they needed. The USM has also created nearly 500 (paper) millionaires.

The Littlewoods Organisation (one of the biggest private companies) had sales in 1984 of more than £1.6 billion! However, most private concerns are small and in the manufacturing sector 80 per cent of them employ fewer than 200 people. Despite their individual small size private companies provide over 30 per cent of the Gross National Product and their contribution to the economy (especially in terms of creating new jobs) is beginning to be recognised.

Over 1.5 million businesses are registered in Britain for VAT and well over 95 per cent of them are small private companies. There are many good reasons why a company should remain private. However, a key factor in deciding to go 'public' is often the need for access to funds which only a wide range of investors can provide.

The ownership of *public companies,* in contrast to that of private companies, is in the hands of anyone who buys the shares. Today more than half the shares of public companies are in the hands of pension funds, insurance companies etc—the institutions. These institutions are of course investing money which has, for the most part, been provided by millions of ordinary people from their savings and pension contributions. Those who invest in such companies as the Halifax, the Prudential and the Abbey National (with its 9 million customers) are indirectly supporting the industrial and commercial life of the nation.

Most public companies are large and employ more than 500 people. Many are active in more than one location. Sometimes each establishment can be a company in its own right. It will then be a *subsidiary,* and its shares will be owned by the *parent* company. In some cases the role of the parent company is not to trade itself but to provide and manage the funds of its subsidiaries. This is called a *holding company*.

Just as some concerns will expand from their original town, so others will develop interests in other countries. Overseas trade may lead to opportunities to manufacture or assemble goods abroad, and for this purpose it may be helpful to establish local subsidiaries. The parent companies are known as *multi-nationals*.

GROUPS WITHIN THE COMPANY

The law recognises three distinct groups of people in a company: shareholders; directors and employees. Those employees who, as executive directors, manage the everyday running of the company may also be shareholders in it and thus fill all three roles!

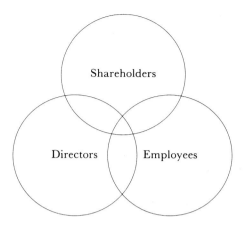

Figure 4

*Shareholders*

The shareholders are the legal owners of the company. As we have seen they can be the great city institutions, other companies or members of the public. The government has total ownership of some state corporations (see below) and has shareholdings in a number of other companies.

Shareholders are more influential in some companies than others; much depends on whether the shares are held in large blocks or small packets. The law requires a meeting of shareholders once a year and other meetings may be necessary to discuss matters affecting the constitution of the company.

Shareholders can expect a return on their investment which takes the form of *dividend*. The size of the dividend depends on how much profit has been made and how much needs to be retained within the business to finance the company's future activities.

*Directors*

The *board of directors* has legal powers and duties. Directors are either *executive* (they work as managers in the business), or *non-executive*. The latter group may be appointed to represent an important interest in the company (eg a bank, major shareholder or parent company), or to provide special expertise.

The chairman of the board is often a non-executive director but, despite this, the chairman will have considerable influence on the composition of the board and will certainly appoint the managing director or chief executive. The latter is responsible for seeing that the company meets its legal obligations and commercial objectives.

The role of the board is to make policy decisions and to see that these are carried out. Its decisions are usually major ones, perhaps involving capital investment in new plant or concerning expansion into other areas of business. The board will deal on its own with relationships with other companies but acquisitions and mergers may require the consent of the shareholders.

The board has a responsibility to act in the interests of the company as a whole. It has no particular or exclusive duty towards any special-interest group—the shareholders, employees, customers or suppliers. Directors are required to display integrity at all times when dealing with the company's affairs and to act in good faith in what they consider is the best interest of the company. They must not make a secret profit out of their job and must not allow themselves to get into a position where their duties and their personal interests conflict. Shares held by directors and their families in the company must be disclosed and in broad terms failure to do so is a criminal offence.

### Employees

The law recognises a company's employees and gives them special rights and protection. A wise company will also recognise the importance of its employees and many companies go beyond the minimum requirements of the law in order to ensure that the company's most important asset is looked after properly.

### PUBLICLY OWNED CORPORATIONS

We have seen that there are 'private' and 'public' companies. Both are owned by shareholders but ownership is a private affair even if the shareholder is one of the great financial institutions. These companies are therefore said to make up the *private sector* of industry.

The *public sector* comprises the state-owned concerns. This would include the electricity and coal industries, the Post Office and the BBC. In place of the articles and memoranda of association the public corporations are established by Parliament.

The day-to-day management of public-sector industries is conducted in much the same way as in the private sector, but decisions reached by the board of directors are sometimes overruled by the government. The handling of public-sector policy is frequently a matter of political debate. For example there is continuous discussion over the extent to which the railway system should be subsidised or which of the public sector organisations should be privatised (eg British Telecom).

## LARGE AND SMALL ORGANISATIONS

It is generally accepted that it is good for a country's industrial base to be made up of a mix of large and small firms. Large companies often rely on small ones to supply them with components, or goods which are needed in the big companies' range of products, but only in small quantities. Generally small companies are quicker on their feet, have lower overheads and are good at low-volume items.

A mix of large and small firms in the economy means that a variety of jobs are available to individuals. However, as production processes become more and more automated the trend is for large firms to be capital intensive. Small firms by contrast are generally labour intensive (ie a high ratio of employees to sales). With the present high level of unemployment government is attempting to encourage job creation in various ways, including assistance to new and small businesses.

In a small business everyone knows each other and a family atmosphere prevails. This has a generally beneficial effect on the individual's attitude to his or her work and statistics indicate that there are fewer stoppages as a result of industrial relations problems in small organisations than there are in larger ones. The problem of making each person feel that his or her contribution is valued increases as an organisation grows in size. Large companies therefore need to take special measures to ensure good employee motivation. Their advantage is that they can often offer employees better training, career prospects, pay, security etc.

Being big can bring economic benefits to a company. The raising of capital to finance large projects becomes easier, and large manufacturing plants are cheaper to run per unit produced. Some activities require plant and investment of such size that only big firms can cope. Thus the manufacturing side of the petro-chemical industry is predominantly made up of large organisations.

# 2

# MARKETING AND SALES

### What is Marketing?

'Marketing' is a much misunderstood term and is often wrongly used. Many—perhaps most—people think that it is another word for selling. Indeed selling *is* part of the marketing activity, but only a part.

*Marketing is the management process responsible for identifying, anticipating and satisfying customer requirements profitably.*

A 'market' is where goods are bought, sold or exchanged. The concept of a market is very old, almost universal, and very familiar to us all. Indeed the word itself is recognisable in most European languages, eg *marché, Markt.* Four components are needed for a market to exist:

1 Buyers—people wishing to acquire goods.
2 Sellers—people wishing to dispose of goods.
3 Goods—to change hands.
4 Money—to exchange for the goods.

'Marketing' comes from the word 'market'. Therefore the key to the proper understanding of the marketing function lies in an understanding of the four components as they affect a company.

The company is the seller. As such it must give careful consideration and attention to the other three components of the market—buyers, goods and money. All of these must be available in the right quantities, at the right time and in the right place.

The buyers are the people who wish to acquire goods, products and services because they need them, or believe they need them. Satisfying the needs of the buyer—the customer—is vital. It can be argued that the main purpose of a company is to secure and keep customers. Hence the expression 'The customer is always right'. Without customers nothing else that the company does is of any value.

What does the buyer want? Some things are essential like food; others, like cosmetics or visits to the cinema, are not strictly necessary; and others, like private planes, are luxuries that few of us will ever own.

If we are unable to satisfy all our requirements we choose between them, selecting the essentials first and working through our personal priorities. In the developed economies of the world most of us can easily afford the basic needs of life—food, shelter and security—and people are able to buy some non-essential items from amongst the many that are available. These things might be physical products, or they could be 'services' like dry-cleaning.

Once basic needs have been satisfied, people choose to buy goods according to what money they have available and how badly they want or need a particular product or service. A company wishing to sell a product must identify which people want it *and* find out how much they are willing to pay for it. Only then can it start to persuade them to buy its goods with any degree of confidence.

We can now see why marketing involves more than just selling. It is concerned in basic policy decisions that will affect the whole running of the company. In order to examine this in greater detail we shall divide the marketing activity into four key areas of interest (which differ from the four components of the market). These are:

1 The market.
2 The product.
3 The contribution to profit.
4 Reaching the customer.

Throughout this chapter we shall be concerned primarily with the 'consumer' market: that is the provision of goods and services to the general public. This area will be familiar to you and will provide use-

# The marketing spectrum

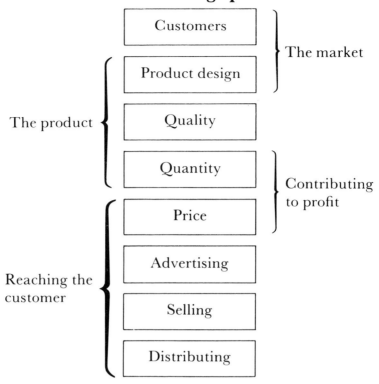

Figure 13 This chart shows the activities and interests of a marketing department, and how the following sections of the chapter divide them under convenient headings. Notice how the sections relate to each other.

---

ful and clearly understandable examples.

All the principles and ideas mentioned are equally applicable to the provision of goods for industry itself. The scale of activity may be different—multi-million-pound oil rigs are not made in great quantity and there aren't many people who want to buy them. Nonetheless the basic facts of marketing hold good, even in the making and selling of the most sophisticated and specialised items.

## The Market

The word 'market' is used by marketing specialists to mean any group of people who are potential purchasers. They buy to satisfy their own needs or on behalf of the organisation that employs them.

In general terms individuals usually buy *consumer* goods and organisations buy *industrial* goods.

The distinction between the two types of purchaser—the two kinds of market—is important to the marketing man, but for our purpose the similarities between the two are more important. At the beginning of the book the importance of *people* in industry was stressed. This point can usefully be made again—it is individuals who make purchasing decisions, not 'companies'.

MARKET RESEARCH
The more a company knows about its market the better. The most significant questions are:

1  How many buyers could need my product; what sort of people are they and where are they?
2  Where and when do they buy goods like ours?
3  How badly is the product needed—what will people pay for it?
4  What is the competition?
5  How can we provide a product that is better than anybody else's?

By answering these questions in a scientific and orderly way companies will seek to assess their market. A vital part of this task is to measure the *trends* as well as the existing situation. The assessment must be done at a reasonable cost. Getting the right information at the right cost is an important exercise in itself. The inquiry process must not go on for ever or final results for action will never be obtained and the cost of the inquiry will escalate. Success will depend on:

1  Asking the right questions.
2  Asking the right people and consulting the right sources of information.

This process is known as *market research*.

Markets containing many potential buyers must be researched selectively. It is time-consuming, costly and generally impractical to question every potential customer. The technique used is to talk to a sample representing a cross-section of the market. It is a well-understood and reliable method, despite the well-publicised failure of election forecasts!

There are many readily available sources of published information which provide facts quickly and easily without going to the cost of interviewing individuals. Government statistics, trade directories and other published data available in libraries are extremely useful. For example, it would be relatively simple to find out how many farmers there are in Great Britain, if one were thinking of selling tractors or agricultural equipment. Similarly, if you were thinking of selling pet food, the number of dogs living in Great Britain can be ascertained from Post Office licence statistics.

An established company will have much useful information on file already. Customer records, sales figures for previous years, information on other company products, and comments made to the salesforce can all be used to good effect.

If these sources cannot provide the answers then there are several methods of questioning people—by sending a questionnaire through the post, phoning, personal interviews, through members of the salesforce visiting potential customers etc.

How and when questions are asked is very important if the answers are to be valid. For example, you would get a very wrong view of how many people are interested in going to football matches if you questioned people in the street at 3 o'clock on a winter Saturday afternoon!

As a result of market research a company can work out what its share of a potential market might be and from this a *sales forecast* and *sales targets* can be produced. These figures in turn will help to determine how much of the product should be made and at what cost.

## The Product

BASIC PRODUCT CHARACTERISTICS AND POSITIONING

A company must try to provide products which satisfy its customers' needs. People buy goods and services for a number of reasons and many factors will influence their decisions. The more obvious characteristics are:

1  Function. You may need something to write with but exactly what do you want it to do? For example, must the writing be permanent or will you want to erase it?
2  Appearance. Patterned wallpaper is a good example of a product that is chosen for its looks. Painted surfaces are just as practical and are usually cheaper, but they do not create as decorative a setting.
3  Price. A family might be able to afford a £200 package holiday, but

not a £2,000 world cruise—however much they'd like to.
4  Status. Status is difficult to quantify but it is a real factor in many
   buyers' minds. Does a Rolls-Royce really function twenty times
   better than a Mini?

To succeed a company must conceive and design products to the
standards of function, appearance and price which appeal to its
chosen market sector—the people to whom it wishes to sell. In order
to reach these customers the product is *positioned* in the market.
Exclusive and expensive products are said to be *up-market* and cheap,
mass-produced goods are described as *down-market*.

PRODUCT LIFE
People's needs and life-styles are changing all the time, slowly in
some cases and quickly in others. Over a period of time changing
needs will produce markets for new products and well-established
products will cease to satisfy and become redundant.

The period of time over which a product appeals to customers is
called the *product life*. Note that this is a technical term used in marketing and does not refer to the useful life of an individual item before
it wears out.

At any given time a product is at a certain point in its life cycle.
Plotted on a graph a typical life cycle looks like that in Fig 14. The
dotted lines show what happens when improvements to the product
or changes in the way it is marketed take place.

Some products tend to have very short lives—moonboots and
skateboards for instance. By contrast carpentry tools change very
little over the years and have very long product lives.

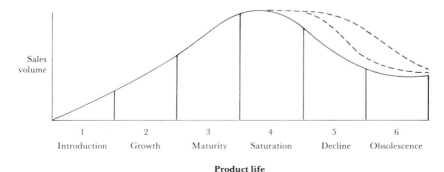

**Product life**

Figure 14

The marketing task is constantly to check changing trends, phasing out dying products and developing new ones.

BRANDED GOODS AND 'OWN LABEL'

Increased mechanisation has enabled companies to manufacture goods in great quantity. This has encouraged standardisation and emphasised the need to plan a smooth flow of production. If products are increasingly uniform the marketing manager will want to try and distinguish his or her company's product from the rest (one tin of baked beans is much like another), so in order to do this the concept of *branding* has developed. The value of branding products as an aid to advertising and sales promotion is now well established.

For example, once upon a time every town and village had its own bakery. Today this is less true; much of the bread we eat is 'branded'—like Mothers Pride and Sunblest.

The cost of 'promoting'—or advertising—the brand can represent a sizeable proportion of the overall cost. The idea is to recover the expense through increased sales, which mean a greater volume of production and therefore lower costs for each item. Promotional costs tend to be highest in the fast-moving consumer market—items like detergent and packaged food which can be identified as those which are most frequently advertised on television.

Over the last twenty-five years there has been a parallel development in the growth of *'retail branding'*: chains such as Tesco and Boots sell a wide range of goods under their own brand name, and Marks & Spencer sells everything under its own 'St Michael' label.

Most of the goods sold in this way are virtually the same as proprietary brands but in a special package. The advantage to retailers is that they can negotiate a particularly attractive price with the maker who is spared the cost of advertising and promotion. This cost saving can be increased by discounts for bulk orders and, in consequence, the consumer benefits from a low retail price. The benefit to manufacturers lies in their ability to forecast production requirements accurately and thereby maximise the use of resources.

## Pricing and Profit

At the beginning of this chapter we saw that a market is made up of four components—buyers, sellers, goods and money. The marketing department of a company must be concerned with all four components—including money. There are few decisions more difficult than getting the price of a service or product right. To see how the selling price can be influenced we must first understand something of the way in which a company's costs are made up. (See also Chapter 2.)

DIRECT AND INDIRECT COSTS

A company makes a profit over a period of time if it earns more than it spends. Its expenses can be divided into two categories.

1 Some of the company's expenditure is directly related to producing the goods it wishes to sell. These are *direct costs* and are mostly laid out on buying raw materials with which to make the products (say steel for car bodies) and on paying the employees who actually make the goods. The term *variable costs* is an alternative description as these costs vary directly with the volume of production (the quantity of goods made).

2 Some expenditure is necessary just for a company to exist and is not directly linked to the number of things made. Office rents and heating, the salaries of general management and the cost of administration and clerical staff are paid for out of this type of expenditure. These are the *indirect costs* of the product. They are also referred to as *fixed costs* or *overheads*.

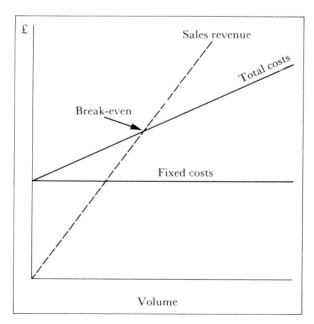

Figure 15

The production manager is responsible for controlling the direct costs. The company's general management controls overheads and by keeping these down can help the profitability of the company.

Fig 15 shows how the direct costs and overheads can be calculated to show the cost price of each unit produced. If a company is making more than one product—say chairs and tables—the overheads will be calculated for each product as a percentage of the company's total overheads bill. These fixed costs are shown by a horizontal line because they are not related to the volume of production. The direct costs rise with volume. At a given selling price it is possible to determine how many units must be made to recover all the costs incurred. Alternatively the lowest acceptable price can be established for a given volume of production. The point at which income matches costs is known as the *break-even point*.

The marketing function can contribute to the control of overhead expenditure (on say the salesforce's wages or advertising campaigns), however marketing's most important influence is not on expenditure but income.

CONTRIBUTION TO OVERHEADS AND PROFIT

The difference between the sales revenue and direct costs 'contributes' to overheads and ultimately to the company's profit. How can the marketing department influence this 'contribution'?

The following example of an imaginary price/volume/profit calculation shows how careful pricing and production of the right volume is essential if the contribution is to be sufficient. The left side of the table shows the prices and how many items can be sold at these different prices. As the price drops so the sales volume increases—but not in ratio. The figures in the middle show the cost of producing the goods and the resulting profit is given on the right-hand side.

The example shows that £110 is the most profitable price for the product. Lowering the price to £100 or £90 decreases profit because the increased volume of sales is insufficient to compensate for the smaller contribution to overheads of each item. If the current price of the goods is £100, then the proper commercial decision would be to raise the price £10, reduce production to 90 units and thus increase profit!

A key function of the marketing department is to provide accurate information about the likely effects of pricing on sales volume. The important lesson to be drawn is that increasing prices will not always increase profitability, nor will increasing production! The equation

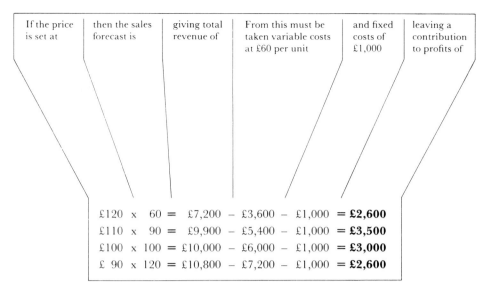

| If the price is set at | then the sales forecast is | giving total revenue of | From this must be taken variable costs at £60 per unit | and fixed costs of £1,000 | leaving a contribution to profits of |
|---|---|---|---|---|---|
| £120 x | 60 = | £7,200 | – £3,600 | – £1,000 | = **£2,600** |
| £110 x | 90 = | £9,900 | – £5,400 | – £1,000 | = **£3,500** |
| £100 x | 100 = | £10,000 | – £6,000 | – £1,000 | = **£3,000** |
| £ 90 x | 120 = | £10,800 | – £7,200 | – £1,000 | = **£2,600** |

Figure 16 Example of a price volume profit calculation

is usually more complex than the example suggests. Often the marketeer will be working against a deadline and he or she may not have all the facts. Some of the facts which are available will be contradictory and in the end the decision to purchase or not will be at the whim of the consumer. How easy, for instance, would it be to predict the effect of changing the quality of the product? This kind of calculation is not made any easier by statistics which indicate that approximately nine out of ten new products fail.

## Reaching the Customer

Having looked at the less well-understood aspects of marketing, we can now examine an aspect which will be more familiar to you—contact with the customer.

ADVERTISING

A key marketing task is to stimulate customers' awareness of their needs and the way in which the company products could help to meet these. This is done by working out 'product characteristics' for each item and presenting them in a way which will appeal to each type of potential buyer. The next step is to draw the likely customers' attention to the product.

This is done through advertising. A company could inform its customers of a new product by individual letter or it could rely on word of mouth. Such methods would be appropriate if the product is to be made in very small numbers for a specialised market. In most cases, however, the company will need to publicise its wares more widely, using every suitable means to reach all potential customers.

When a product is first introduced a major part of the advertising effort will be put into telling people it exists and informing them of its special characteristics. These are called its *unique selling points*.

Advertising does not replace the salesforce but it will help to make selling easier. If a sound advertising campaign has already told potential customers about the product their interest will have been aroused. They will be anxious to see an example and ready to discuss its suitability.

After a product is established in the market it is necessary to continue to remind customers about it and this is an ideal role for conventional advertising. The advertisements themselves will be designed to support the sales team and will relate the product to changing market conditions. Consider for example a washing machine that was introduced last year as the very latest thing in home laundering. This year the advertising plan could be to promote it as a well-tried and proven device which will be more reliable than its newer rivals.

Before deciding on any advertising campaign it is vital to establish the aim of the promotion. Is it to sustain or to increase sales? If sales are to be increased should this be done by finding more customers or by increasing the uses of the product? A good example of the latter approach was the development of kitchen foil from a simple aid for baking to a multi-purpose wrapping material—including use as a thermal blanket for runners at the finish of marathons!

*Media*

There are two components in an advertising campaign—the *message* and the *medium*. Some aspects connected with how the message might be planned have been touched on above. Having decided what to say, the seller must consider where to say it.

The main options are:

1  Television and radio.
2  Newspapers and periodicals.
3  Specialist trade magazines.
4  Hoardings.

## Advertising Media

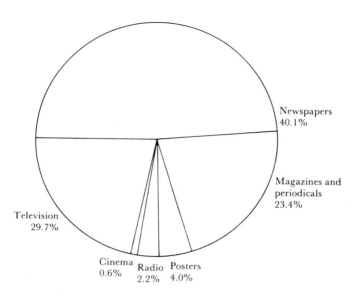

Figure 17 This chart shows how the total money spent on advertising is divided between the various media

Who are the potential customers or 'target audience'? They could be other companies, householders, teenagers, or any other group of people.

People's reading, viewing and travelling habits have been very carefully studied. Market researchers have categorised all of us according to our spending power, education, hobbies and habits. Therefore the advertising message can be directed at any particular group of people with surprising accuracy.

Even on a personal level we recognise the most cost-effective way of drawing attention to the things we want to sell. You wouldn't hire a hoarding in the high street to advertise your old bike. It is similarly no accident that there are few adverts for soap powder in *Motor Sport*! These are crude examples of a skill that has been highly developed.

### Advertising agencies

The skills of the advertiser are too specialised for most companies to employ their own. The *agency* system has been developed over the years so that a business need only hire the services of an expert for

the minimum time required. Even within agencies there are specialists such as copywriters, artists and designers.

The agencies' services will not necessarily be confined to the task
of advertising. Their special knowledge of the psychology of the
customer may enable them to make an important contribution to
such things as packaging or even the naming of a new product.

DISTRIBUTION

The paths by which goods get from the factory to the customer are
called *channels of distribution*. Getting the product to the customer is
part of the marketing function—part of the problem of 'satisfying the
needs of the market'. Arrangements for the physical handling of
goods are dealt with by specialists, but the pattern of distribution is
in the hands of the marketing department.

It is common for industrial products to be sold by the maker direct
to the user, whilst consumer goods are more usually distributed
through retail shops. The maker could supply the shops direct but to
do this the company would need a large salesforce. An alternative is
to use wholesalers who buy in bulk and can be served by a small
salesforce. The wholesalers' charge (or *mark-up*) is added on to the
manufacturer's price so there is no cost advantage to the buyer but
stocks are held close to the retail outlet and this speeds up service.

SELLING

Marketing is about providing what the customer wants. Selling is
about getting customers to buy what the company has.

The manufacturer's customer may not be the end user of the
product. There could be a wholesaler or retailer helping to progress
the goods from factory to final customer. The marketing manager
will wish to influence this member of the chain and may do so by
advertising, fixing attractive discounts, giving incentives or by providing quality and good service.

Members of the salesforce in consumer goods industries are essentially concerned with selling finished products. This is not always the
case with *industrial* selling. Industrial sales staff are trained, for the
most part, to sell raw materials or components to professional
buyers. They are more likely to be technically qualified and are often
required to advise customers on the right product (out of a wide
range of goods) to fill a particular need.

A good salesforce is an important asset to any company. They
must know the product they are selling, understand the customer's

needs and be able to communicate the benefits of the company's products. They must be persistent but not rude, personable but not 'flash', energetic and resourceful. The job is amongst the most demanding in business and, recognising this, many companies pay their full-time sales staff a good basic salary linked to an incentive scheme, based on the volume of sales achieved. This *commission* element will vary according to the type of product, and between companies. Some salespeople prefer to operate as *agents* and are paid solely on a commission basis.

The products produced by industry are either items to be purchased by other companies for further processing, or they are 'finished goods' destined for the consumer. In the next section we will look at the different ways in which these finished goods can reach the ordinary customer.

## The Retail Trade

SHOPS

Everybody is familiar with buying from shops, but not everybody stops to think what the function of a shop is, or to notice the changes in retailing that are steadily taking place.

Retailing looks so easy, yet many skills are involved. Goods must be selected which will appeal to the shop's particular type of customer; pricing must be competitive; the site must be carefully chosen so that the costs are in line with expected trade; the shop must be designed to attract people inside; goods must be displayed so as to invite purchase; staff have to be recruited; and the business must be run so that a reasonable profit is made—the task of management. If the retailer does all this well the shop will provide satisfaction to its customers and work for its employees.

Every year many small shops close because they are not as efficient as chains of similar shops, which can often provide a wider range of goods. Efficiency enables prices to be lowered or service to be improved or a combination of both. That is why the traditional grocer's shop, owned by an individual shopkeeper, is slowly disappearing and giving way to huge supermarkets owned by public companies.

The city centre, as the hub of shopping, is being challenged by the out-of-town hypermarket. Many people now have their own transport and prefer to travel by car to a site where there is ample parking. In response, city centres have been redeveloped with multi-storey car parks and covered, air-conditioned shopping precincts.

Retailing provides jobs as well as a means of purchasing goods. Around 2.25 million people derive their livelihood from retailing and this represents over 10 per cent of the working population.

Shops provide the essential link between factories and consumers. Life would be extremely difficult without them!

MAIL ORDER

Mail order is a form of retailing in which goods are sold through catalogues and these act as a form of 'shop window' for the businesses which produce the catalogues. In total, mail order sales approximately equal sales through department stores.

Most large mail order companies issue two catalogues a year—one in January for spring and summer and one in July for autumn and winter. Many items are common to both issues but there are seasonal variations—especially in the fashion sections. The catalogues consist of up to 1,000 pages and offer a range of goods comparable with that carried by a large department store. They display all the items in full colour together with descriptions, sizes, colours, prices and the various payment terms.

In the United Kingdom, mail order companies sell mostly through part-time agents, generally housewives, whom they recruit by advertising in newspapers and magazines. Each agent earns commission—usually 10 per cent of sales—and one of the pleasant aspects of the job is the social enjoyment of selling to family and friends.

There are benefits too for a customer buying goods by mail order. Primarily there is the convenience of shopping at home with goods being delivered to the door at no charge. All items are sent on approval and customers are able to return them, usually at the company's expense, should they not be suitable. Everything is offered on credit and the intention is for these credit prices to be the same as the cash prices in the shops.

The telephone is rapidly replacing the post as a means of communication, especially for the placing of orders. Deliveries, which usually take a few days, are speeded up and customers can check whilst they are on the phone that the items they want are in stock.

Because mail order companies handle goods in central warehouses, they are able to take advantage of the latest mechanical handling systems and computer control in various areas. Indeed the whole mail order business has developed on the back of modern technology.

DIRECT MAIL

Selling by direct mail is expanding rapidly. Products of many kinds are offered for sale through advertisements, which up till recently, were published in newspapers and magazines. Increasingly, however, the trend is for these advertisements to come through the letter-box in the form of a letter, leaflet or even a catalogue. Here again the computer is influencing development because computers make it possible to send individual letters to people with a likely interest in the product. For instance, lawn-mowers can be advertised in direct mail shots sent to people known to have gardens.

The customer who wishes to purchase can usually order by telephone or letter and payment is made in advance, either by cheque or charging the cost to a credit account. Frequently deliveries take up to a month.

## What is Selling?

People employed in the sales area are normally required because the product or service can only be successfully sold through the medium of a person to person meeting. Retailing has just been discussed and although retail sales people in the best stores are skilled and trained, they operate in a controlled environment and the customer comes to them.

At the heart of any commercial activity there are two operations—producing the goods (or services) and selling them. Of these two only sales is common to the service sector and manufacture. The sales function is a crucial area for any business and yet the myth persists that only fast-talking, rather unreliable and somewhat brash individuals will make suitable sales people. Nothing could be more dangerous to a business or further from the truth. Selling in industry is about building a relationship with the potential buyer and if the business in question is worth thousands of pounds then the only possible relationship is one of trust. The higher the stake the higher the qualities and professionalism required.

This short review of the sales function deals principally with the sales person who is operating individually and is usually (though not always) on a territory given to him or her by their employer. Territories are frequently defined geographically but they can also be arranged by customer or type of customer. The degree of organisation and control varies enormously with the size of the company and type of product and market. Frequently sales people are organised in teams under the control of an Area Manager or Field Sales Manager.

The task of sales people is to obtain orders for their company's products (or services) in the right quantity and at the right time in order to meet their share of the company's budget. Normally the product has to be sold at the company's stated (sometimes published) price. However some sales people do become more involved in more detailed negotiation on matters such as price, delivery and time scale. This could happen for example when a sales person is negotiating for a repair and maintenance contract in a power station or continuous process plant. In such circumstances the shutdown period is very costly to the customer and performance within a given time scale may matter more than price. A simpler example might be the provision of double glazing for a private home. In this situation the sales person frequently acts as the leader of a negotiating team which may include Contracts Manager, Designer or Surveyor.

QUALIFICATIONS
The degree of formal or technical education needed by a sales person depends on the product and the market which is being served. For example selling an integrated and computerised office system might require a qualified accountant or Business Studies graduate. Selling equipment for a continuous process plant in the Chemical industry would almost certainly require a qualified Chemical Engineer. On the other hand there are many conventional products and services such as office furniture, insurance, printing or factory equipment where people of modest academic achievement may make highly rewarding and successful careers in the Sales Division. Companies who have a clear understanding of how important marketing and selling are to the successful running of their business give good sales training. Sales people need to be highly motivated with acceptable personalities, a degree of optimism, courage and sufficient self-management to organise and plan their own activities. This will enable them to maximise selling time (ie time in front of the customer) and to minimise costs. It is often a lonely and tiring existence since not everybody wants to buy and constant travel is a feature of the lifestyle.

Thus selling is both a highly skilled and highly organised activity which is crucial to the successful achievement of a company's objectives. Most salespeople love their work since the satisfaction of making a sale after many hours work is considerable. Although every new customer is in fact the result of good teamwork, success in selling can feel very personal.

# The Skills Required

In modern highly competitive conditions sales people need to be knowledgeable and skilled in three main areas. If you wanted to go into sales and be successful you would need:

PRODUCT KNOWLEDGE

A detailed knowledge of the products or services which the company offers. This is essential if you are to have the necessary confidence and skill to make good presentations to a wide range of potential customers. Most companies give training in this area.

INDUSTRY KNOWLEDGE

To be able to recognise the opportunity for a sale you need to have a good knowledge of the customers who make up the market. In addition you should know as much as possible about your competitors so that when making a case you can emphasize the strong points of your proposition. This needs to be expressed in terms of the needs of each potential customer so that he or she can feel they are being offered a 'benefit'.

Your knowledge of any given market will increase with experience, provided you are dedicated to the task of gathering the necessary information.

SALES KNOWLEDGE

Good sales technique distinguishes the skilled and successful sales person from the average. Sales technique can be taught and you will need your share of training. Increasingly companies employing a sales force also employ a sales training specialist or buy in the services of a sales training company. Your sales training programme should include some or all of the following elements:

1  The company's sales policy.
2  The company's sales training policy.
3  Planning and territory coverage. This includes detailed information on planning procedures for the territory, the week's work and the day's work.
4  The planning and structure of a sales interview.
5  Training in presentation skills.
6  Telephone technique for obtaining interviews.
7  Relevant financial matters. For example any hire purchase,

credit facilities or financial packages. Rules for dealing with discounts.

8  Company reporting procedures.

The sales function is generally populated with people who are highly motivated, energetic and good at getting on with others. It is a demanding area and not one for the faint-hearted.

# 3
# FINANCE

### The Money-Go-Round

Before a company can start to operate it needs money to pay for its work-force, materials and machinery. These resources can all be expressed in financial terms (a machine is worth £x, and people cost £y per hour). Money, which is readily quantified, is therefore a useful common denominator. It is used to express the company's needs and tends to be used as a yardstick for all aspects of its performance.

Some understanding of the way in which industry acquires and uses its cash is therefore essential to a general appreciation of the subject.

Over the years accountants have built up a mystique about their work. They use jargon and make complex financial arrangements. Most non-accountants think that world of finance and accounting is beyond their understanding! The facts are less daunting than they appear: money comes into and flows out of companies; the 'accounts' explain what has been happening and what the present position is.

In the following sections we shall be considering various aspects of the 'money-go-round' or the 'circulation of capital', which is illustrated in Fig 5. The terms used are not at all complicated and the arrows show clearly what is coming in and what is going out.

For convenience Fig 5 shows a complete cycle. No time scale is

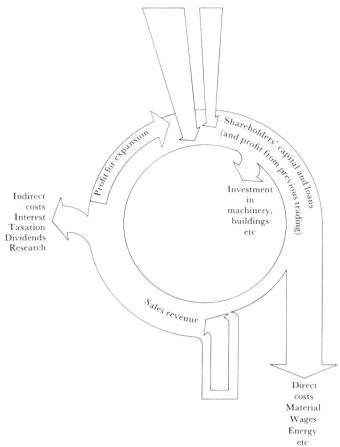

Figure 5

shown—it could be a week, or a year, or the entire life of the company. Indeed in reality several activities will probably be going on at the same time and the picture would not be quite so simple. Nonetheless the system shown holds good for the activities of every enterprise whether industrial or commercial, large or small.

## Sources of Finance

A business needs money to pay for its buildings, machinery, raw materials, stocks and employees.

In Fig 5 two sources of finance are shown, namely: *capital*, provided by its shareholders (the owners); and *loans* (usually from banks). A third source is also included, which is often overlooked. This is the *profit from previous trading* which is used by the company to pay for growth, to repay loans or to finance normal trading.

If we expand that part of the picture more detail can be shown, and it is possible to see a fourth source of money—the credit allowed by suppliers.

Whatever its source, the money available to the company is considered to be a *liability* in that it must be repaid if the company ever comes to an end and is wound up. It is money owed.

SHAREHOLDERS FUNDS

When a company is registered it must state the maximum figure it plans to get from the shareholders. This is called its *authorised share capital*. The amount the shareholders actually provide is called the *issued share capital*, and the company can go on offering shares until the authorised share capital level is reached.

Sometimes it is possible to increase the authorised share capital. However, the need for more finance forces the company to decide whether to borrow the money from the bank (better for short-term loans) or to issue shares. The latter course leads to a further choice; between remaining private or going public. Although a public company does not have to be quoted on the Stock Exchange it may find it advantageous to seek a listing in order to find a market for its shares and to raise money.

Before a business can get started money has to be found so that the company can buy the things it needs to operate. Sole traders, partnerships and limited companies get off the ground through the owners putting their own money into the enterprise. We need, however, to differentiate between the private limited company and the public limited company (PLC or plc). Both raise money through the issue of shares but the main difference is that private companies cannot offer shares to or raise money from the public.

|  | *Private Limited Company* | *Public Limited Company* |
| --- | --- | --- |
| *Number of Shareholders* | 2 upwards (no limit) | 2 upwards (no limit) |
| *Who receives the profits* | Shared between shareholders | Shared between shareholders |
| *Limited liability?* | Yes | Yes |
| *Sources of capital* | Personal savings, bank loans, suppliers' credit, grants, sale of shares privately | As Private Limited Company, plus sale of shares publicly and raising money |

| *Usual size* | Small/medium | Medium/large |
|---|---|---|
| *Denoted as* | Limited (Ltd) | PLC or plc |

LOANS AND BORROWINGS

Loans are usually obtained from banks, but there are other lending institutions. Loans can range from a bank overdraft, which is usually for short-term requirements, to medium- and long-term arrangements. These are loans designed to cover periods of up to twenty years or more and normally provide finance for specific projects.

The usual and most important sources for medium- and long-term loans for companies are:

1 The major 'high street' banks such as National Westminster, Barclays, Lloyds and Midland.
2 Merchant banks and suppliers of venture capital such as Investors in Industry Limited.
3 Insurance companies, building societies and other institutions such as pension funds.
4 Public funds from various government departments (eg the Department of Trade and Industry), various development agencies and other funding such as the Loan Guarantee Scheme and the Business Expansion Scheme.

In most cases loans from banks or institutions are only given if the company provides a 'security' for them: in simple terms there must be some asset which the borrower promises to hand over if the loan cannot be repaid in any other way. It might be a building but needless to say the same asset cannot be offered as security to more than one lender!

PROFIT

Once a company is trading its profit provides another source of finance. After meeting tax obligations some profit may be distributed to the shareholders at so much per share. This is their reward for, and return on, the capital they put into the business. The remainder of the profit will be retained by the company to help finance further expansion or the continuation of trading.

The importance of profit as a source of finance cannot be over-emphasised. It is the primary source of cash to pay for growth or expansion. Contrary to popular belief companies do not collect profits in the bank as a private hoard of wealth.

CREDIT

A company's suppliers can also provide finance. If a company orders and receives goods, but delays payment for two months, it has obtained two months' credit. During this period of credit the goods might well be resold (at a profit). The cash received can then be used to pay the supplier and the company has thus been able to trade profitably without using any of its own capital.

When sales personnel negotiate with a customer an important part of their task is to agree a price for the goods *and* the terms of business, ie the time allowed before the customer must pay the bill. Export orders in particular must be carefully negotiated. Not only must the credit offered be considered, but also the rate of exchange. The relative values of currencies change and could mean a loss if the change is unfavourable.

The giving and obtaining of credit are key factors in ensuring that a company trades successfully; those businesses which have a large number of customers may find it necessary and profitable to set up and maintain a special department to control credit.

## Uses of Finance

We have now seen where a company's money comes from. How is it used?

Money is spent on all the things that are needed to make the company work. They are then known as *assets*—they can be sold off to repay debts or liabilities. The assets include machinery, materials, buildings that are owned, and any money in the bank. They can be considered under three headings:

1 Fixed assets—items the company can keep long term (see page 52).
2 Personnel.
3 Current assets—items the company can sell (see page 52).

In Fig 5 the outgoings of the company were shown under slightly different headings. Again if the picture is enlarged we can see more detail which will enable us to relate the headings to the list above.

FIXED ASSETS

Before a company can start business it has to acquire the equipment it needs to enable it to operate. In the case of a manufacturing company the machinery could be very expensive indeed and it must have somewhere to house the equipment and the whole operation. It may

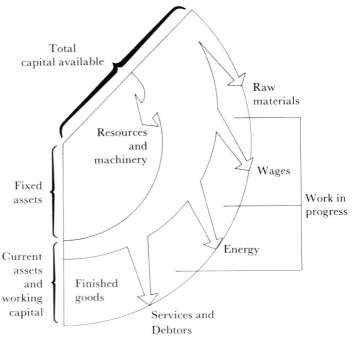

Figure 6

also have to purchase lorries or cars for the salesforce.

These items are said to be *fixed assets:* they are used for the manufacture of the company's products and for carrying out its daily business. In the ordinary course of events they are not for resale. In Fig 5 they are represented in the centre of the circulation and you can think of them as being the hub around which the business operates, for if they were taken away the business would collapse.

PERSONNEL

Money is required to hire people with the necessary skills to undertake the many tasks involved in making and selling goods. Staff are also required for management and administrative jobs. They will be paid weekly wages or monthly salaries and expect these whether the company is going through a good period or not.

When recruiting someone these days companies generally have to allow about 15 per cent of salary to cover National Insurance and pension contributions. Hence someone earning £6,000 probably costs the company nearly £7,000 per annum.

People must be trained, perhaps through apprenticeship schemes or by sending them on courses. They need facilities such as canteens and the security of a pension plan. The company must therefore invest in people as if they were fixed assets.

Unfortunately investment in training is not shown in the accounts as an asset because it cannot be sold or converted back into cash. So in Fig 6 the cost of training and the other facilities provided for the work-force are all included under 'wages'.

CURRENT ASSETS

These are the items belonging to the business which can readily be turned into cash. In Fig 6 they are represented by the headings 'raw materials', 'wages', 'energy', 'services' and finished goods'.

1  Raw materials. During the manufacturing cycle a company will purchase raw materials some of which will not be used immediately and will be held as 'stock'. Materials are called from stock into the production department to be worked on in accordance with pro-duction programmes. Because the stock has been paid for it is costing the company money.
2  Wages. Buying, handling and processing raw materials costs money and, in addition, wages must be paid; quite apart, as we have seen, from the hidden cost of training and staff facilities.
3  Energy. Gas, electricity and fuel oil will be used to work machines and to heat buildings.
4  Services. A company has to spend money on various 'services' to support this work. They include insurance, telephone and telex, post, audit, vehicle repairs, and rates for local authority services.
5  Debtors. Money owed to the company.
6  Finished goods. Perhaps the best source of potential cash, even if they have to be sold cheaply.

All these outgoings are paying for work which is adding value to the materials as they are fashioned into the finished product. Par-tially completed work is often referred to as *work-in-progress*.

Like raw materials and finished goods, work-in-progress can have a price put on it. It is an asset that could be sold, but for the time being work-in-progress has simply cost the company money.

As production work continues the work-in-progress goes on increasing in value until it becomes the finished product. Unless items have been made to a specific order they will probably be put aside as finished goods stock awaiting buyers. Until they are sold they will continue to cost money.

When the product is sold orders are met from finished stocks. In practice only retail business is conducted for cash and the normal practice in manufacturing is for the account to be settled in about thirty days. The customer is a *debtor* until the bill is paid and some comment on the importance of controlling credit has already been made under the section headed 'Credit'.

In Fig 6 we saw money leaving the company under a series of headings. In accountancy language the money has been spent on 'current assets' which are represented by:

1  Raw material stocks.
2  Work-in-progress.
3  Finished goods.
4  Debtors.

Current assets will also include any cash that the company holds—at the bank or on its premises.

The money needed to pay for the current assets—the money that has been moving round the outside of the diagram—is known as *working capital*.

## Making a Profit

Making a profit is essential to the survival of industry. Fig 7 shows money coming into the company from the sale of its goods. The income covers the costs incurred in making the goods and any excess over those costs is shown as profit.

This is too simple a statement to be strictly true. The company will have to spend money on activities and items that are not directly related to the production and sale of its products. We have already seen that training of staff and the provision of facilities for them are among these items. Money must also be set aside to replace machinery and equipment as it wears out, to pay for research and development of new and improved products, and perhaps to meet claims made under the guarantee the company offers on its products. These costs are called *general overheads*.

So Fig 7 only shows the 'trading profit'. Many companies make more than one product. Each is accounted for separately so that its performance can be measured, and each contributes its trading profit to the company. The general overheads such as those just mentioned are paid for out of this *contribution to overheads*.

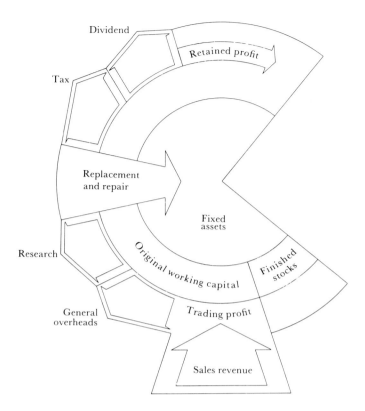

Figure 7

After provision has been made for general overheads we are nearer to seeing a true profit but, before any dividend can go to the shareholders, corporation tax must be paid as well as the interest on any loans. The standard rate for corporation tax is 30-40 per cent of profits, but this will vary over the years, in line with government policy. Even after this there are other calls on the profit. As we have already seen profit is an important source of capital and one which is normally used to pay fr the expansion of the business.

Having seen the need for capital to start a business the cost of expansion can be imagined as being of a similar order. One of the main difficulties being faced by British industry is a lack of sufficient profit—which makes it difficult to invest in the future.

## Presenting the Accounts

THE LEGAL REQUIREMENT
As a result of trading, money is continually coming into a business

from various sources and being converted into assets which are 'fixed' if they are not to be resold and 'current' if they are. A record of all transactions is kept, but from time to time the management and shareholders will need to review the financial situation without wading through a mass of records.

In order to see exactly where the money has come from and where it has gone to, a *balance sheet* can be drawn up which identifies the value of the items in each of these categories.

The balance sheet is a picture of a company's affairs at a given time and like a photograph it lacks 'movement'. To see how the company is performing additional information is needed and the most useful documents in this respect are the *profit and loss account* and the *source and use of funds statement*.

Companies are required by law to produce these records and statements. They must be subjected to a formal examination or *audit* to determine their accuracy. Auditing is carried out by independent qualified accountants. Their task is to verify that the assets and liabilities are as stated and to examine the methods of accounting being used. A good system of bookkeeping will not only include the proper checks and safeguards to prevent fraud but also reduce the need for a detailed check of all transactions.

The law does not require sole traders to present their accounts in the same formal way as limited companies. Nonetheless accounts must be kept for tax purposes and a sole trader would be foolish to neglect the benefits of disciplined financial forecasting and budgeting.

ACCOUNTANTS

The accountant is concerned with all aspects of a company's operation, from raising the initial capital to accounting for profits (or losses).

Before a person can claim to be an accountant he or she must be formally qualified. There are three main types of qualified accountant: chartered accountants; certified accountants; and cost and management accountants.

*Chartered accountants* may work in many different capacities: as part of a company's team of cost and management accountants; as independent auditors examining the accounts; and, frequently, within companies in a general management role because of their specialised knowledge of accounting practice.

*Certified accountants* have the same statutory rights to act as independent auditors as chartered accountants but the majority of them work in companies as part of the cost and management accounts team.

*Cost and management accountants* are concerned primarily with assessing the day-to-day financial performance of an enterprise. Details of their work are discussed in the next section.

THE BALANCE SHEET (Fig 8)
The balance sheet summarises financial affairs at a given date, usually the end of a company's trading year. It acts as verification that all transactions have been recorded correctly. If it does not balance there is an error somewhere in the system of recording. Balanced books are therefore a primary safeguard against fraud.

The main elements of the balance sheet are as follows:

1 Where the money has come from (ie liabilities):
   (a) Shareholders' funds.
   (b) Loans.
   (c) Profits retained in the business.
   (d) 'Current' liabilities.

2 Where the money has gone to (ie assets):
   (a) Fixed assets.
   (b) Current assets: stocks; work-in-progress; debtors; cash.

**Also Furniture Limited**
Balance Sheet as at 31 December 1986

|  | £000's Cost or valuation | Aggregate depreciation | 31 Dec 1986 | 31 Dec 1985 |
|---|---|---|---|---|
| **Fixed Assets** | | | | |
| Freehold property | 4,257 | – | 4,257 | 3,974 |
| Long leasehold | 774 | – | 774 | 774 |
| Plant and machinery | 11,193 | 5,251 | 5,942 | 4,666 |
| Motor vehicles | 136 | 29 | 107 | 149 |
| | 16,360 | 5,280 | 11,080 | 9,563 |
| **Current Assets** | | | | |
| Stocks and work-in-progress at cost or realisable value | | | 7,488 | 7,073 |
| Debtors | | | 7,865 | 7,009 |
| Cash at bank and in hand | | | 86 | 51 |
| | | | 15,439 | 14,133 |

**Current Liabilities**

| | | | |
|---|---|---|---|
| Bank overdrafts | | 2,502 | 347 |
| Creditors | | 7,332 | 7,171 |
| Current taxation | | 1,021 | 1,001 |
| Dividends | | 221 | 135 |
| | | 11,076 | 8,654 |
| Net Current Assets | | 4,363 | 5,479 |
| **Total Net Assets** | | 15,443 | 15,042 |

**Represented by:**

| Share Capital | Authorised | Issued | Issued |
|---|---|---|---|
| Ordinary shares of £1 each | 3,700 | 2,413 | 2,413 |
| 7½% preference shares of £1 each | 300 | 208 | 208 |
| | 4,000 | 2,621 | 2,621 |
| Reserves | | 10,822 | 10,421 |
| Loans | | 2,000 | 2,000 |
| **Capital Employed** | | 15,433 | 15,042 |

Figure 8

Current assets (see page 33) less current liabilities (such as creditors, tax not yet paid and any other temporary overdraft) create the *working capital* of the company.

Fig 8 is an example of a simplified balance sheet for a fictitious company. Note that the conventional layout reverses the order in which its elements have been discussed above.

THE PROFIT AND LOSS ACCOUNT (Fig 9)
The profit and loss account is a statement showing the results of an organisation's trading and other activities over a period of time, usually one year.

The form of profit and loss account shown here complies with the requirements of the Companies Acts. There are many possible layouts but the key elements are:

1 Turnover, or the total receipts from sales.
2 Profit (before taxation).
3 Appropriations of profit (taxation and dividends).
4 Unappropriated profits—transferred to reserves on the balance sheet.

**Also Furniture Limited**
Profit and Loss Account for the year
ended 31 December 1986

| | | £000's 1986 | | 1985 |
|---|---|---|---|---|
| **Turnover** | | 39,887 | | 33,019 |
| Profit before depreciation | | 3,200 | | 3,318 |
| Depreciation | | 1,036 | | 812 |
| Trading profit | | 2,164 | | 2,506 |
| After charging: | | | | |
| Hire of vehicles and equipment | 81 | | 76 | |
| Auditors' remuneration | 44 | | 43 | |
| Directors' remuneration | 123 | | 103 | |
| | 248 | | 222 | |
| Interest | | 382 | | 320 |
| Profit before taxation | | 1,782 | | 2,186 |
| Taxation | | 940 | | 1,091 |
| | | 842 | | 1,095 |
| Preference dividends | | 16 | | 16 |
| | | 826 | | 1,079 |
| Ordinary dividends | | 425 | | 253 |
| Transfer to reserves | | 401 | | 826 |

Figure 9

Note that expenditure is not shown (except those items which have
to be disclosed by law, eg directors' salaries) but it can be discovered
by subtracting profit from turnover.

SOURCE AND USE OF FUNDS STATEMENT (Fig 10)
This document, as its title suggests, sets out to explain where funds
were obtained and to what use they have been put since the previous
balance sheet. The source and use of funds statement can throw
much light on what has happened in an organisation over a given
period of time.

**Also Furniture Limited**
Source and Use of Funds for the Year
ended 31 December 1986

| | £000's 1986 | 1985 |
|---|---|---|
| Source of funds | | |
| Trading profit | 2,164 | 2,506 |
| Depreciation | 1,036 | 812 |
| | 3,200 | 3,318 |

| Use of funds | | |
|---|---:|---:|
| Stocks and work-in-progress | 415 | 328 |
| Debtors | 856 | 503 |
| Creditors | (161) | (92) |
| | 1,110 | 739 |
| Purchase of fixed assets | 2,553 | 1,182 |
| Dividends | 355 | 218 |
| Taxation | 920 | 847 |
| Interest | 382 | 320 |
| | 5,320 | 3,306 |
| Net cash flow | (2,120) | 12 |
| Movement in net liquid funds | | |
| Bank overdrafts | (2,155) | (27) |
| Cash at bank and in-hand | 35 | 15 |
| Increase in net borrowings | (2,120) | 12 |

Figure 10

## Cost and Management Accounting

Cost and management accounts follow no fixed form and are not required by law. They are designed to help management by reducing the risks in decision-making and by monitoring performance. These aims are achieved by reference to the three main elements of the cost and management accountant's work:

1 The budget—broken down into the several parts discussed below.
2 Actual results.
3 Differences (or *variances*) from budget. By highlighting the variances between actual and plan (and by bringing these to the attention of management) the accountant is able to play an important part in the task of getting performance into line with plans.

THE BUDGET (see glossary)
Just as the Chancellor of the Exchequer presents the annual *budget* before the beginning of the fiscal year, a company puts together its forecast of income and expenditure for the coming twelve months. In difficult times a second or third budget may be needed. Managers at all levels are required to provide estimates of expenditure and income for their departments. These are compiled, often by the management

accountant, and presented to the directors for approval. When agreed the budget becomes the yardstick by which the day-to-day performance of the company during the next trading year is measured. The main components of a typical budget are set out below.

*Operating budget*
The operating budget is in effect a forecast profit and loss account. It sets out expected sales revenue (less costs of sales and overheads), net operating results and net profit before taxation. It is often referred to as the profit plan.

*A forecast of product profitability*
This is a supporting document to the operating statement and sets out what profit is expected from each product or division. The use of the word profit in this context can be misleading and is usually replaced by 'margin' or 'contribution'. Each activity of a company should operate profitably, but the *margin* by which its income exceeds expenditure is said to *contribute* to the company's income as well as the cost of support functions eg training, welfare, administration.

The excess of the total of *contributions* over expenditure on these general overheads is the company's profit. One of the main uses of the product profitability forecast is that it focuses the attention of management upon the variable costs of each product group—mainly sales, material and labour. An example is shown in Fig 11.

The significant features to emerge from the example are:

1 'Factored lines' (ie goods made by another manufacturer for you) produce a gross margin of only 28 per cent whilst own manufacture gives 46 per cent. If the enterprise has limited cash resources then own manufacture should have priority even though stools and desks are making a useful contribution to overheads and profit.
2 There is a difference of up to 10 per cent in the gross margins on own manufacture products. Priority should therefore be given to tables and beds if production resources are limited. Alternatively there may be scope for increasing the selling price of the chairs in order to improve margins.

**Also Furniture Limited**
Forecast of Product Profitability
£000's

| Product | Sales | Direct cost of sales | | | Gross margin | Percentage | | |
|---|---|---|---|---|---|---|---|---|
| | | Raw materials | Labour | Total | | Gross margin of sales | Sales mix | Margin mix |
| **Own manufacture** | | | | | | | | |
| Chairs | 660 | 190 | 195 | 385 | 275 | 42 | 38 | 36 |
| Tables | 740 | 194 | 178 | 372 | 368 | 50 | 42 | 48 |
| Beds | 100 | 36 | 12 | 48 | 52 | 52 | 6 | 7 |
| Total | 1500 | 420 | 385 | 805 | 695 | 46 | 86 | 91 |
| **Factored** | | | | | | | | |
| Stools | 190 | 142 | – | 142 | 48 | 25 | 11 | 6 |
| Desks | 60 | 38 | – | 38 | 22 | 37 | 3 | 3 |
| Total | 250 | 180 | – | 180 | 70 | 28 | 14 | 9 |
| TOTAL | 1750 | 600 | 385 | 985 | 765 | 44 | 100 | 100 |

Figure 11

*Research and development budget*

Company policy will dictate what is to be spent on research and development for new products and techniques. Plans in this area will often stem from the requirements of the marketing department and an overall budget for research and development will be allocated between:

1  The payment of salaries and other fixed outgoings.
2  Specific projects.

*Capital expenditure budget*

Fixed assets involve the expenditure of capital which means that money will become tied up in buildings, plant, land etc. In contrast revenue expenditure is directly incurred in daily operations (eg raw materials, wages and other overheads). An organisation needs to plan for the replacement of existing assets either because they will have worn out or because they are likely to become obsolete. Furthermore an organisation may wish to increase its fixed assets to cater for expansion.

*Cash flow forecast*

This last component of the budget is perhaps the most important. It shows on a weekly or monthly basis the income expected against likely expenditure and indicates how the flow of cash in and out of the company will affect its bank balance.

Cash flow problems are all to do with timing. Small and new businesses are particularly vulnerable to the problem, and shortage of cash is still the principal reason for companies failing. Many go under despite good products and reasonable prospects.

Although the results of trading may offer the forecast of a good profit the money may not be coming in until the end of the accounting period. Thus the trader must ensure that there is sufficient cash to pay immediate bills.

For example a builder might take a year to build a house but will not be able to sell it or receive any income until it is complete. Cash

**Cash Flow Forecast**

|  | £000's July | August | Sept | Total |
|---|---|---|---|---|
| **Receipts** | | | | |
| Cash from sales | 120.3 | 40.5 | 75.2 | 236.0 |
| Other income | 9.2 | 4.2 | 5.0 | 18.4 |
|  | 129.5 | 44.7 | 80.2 | 254.4 |
| **Payments** | | | | |
| Materials from suppliers | 50.6 | 27.0 | 70.4 | 148.0 |
| Wages and salaries | 13.4 | 15.0 | 13.6 | 42.0 |
| Insurances | – | 5.0 | – | 5.0 |
| Rates | 10.0 | – | – | 10.0 |
| Other overheads | 13.0 | 11.0 | 12.0 | 36.0 |
| Capital expenditure | 5.0 | 8.0 | 2.0 | 15.0 |
| VAT | – | – | 15.0 | 15.0 |
| Dividends | 4.0 | – | – | 4.0 |
| Corporation tax | 18.0 | – | – | 18.0 |
|  | 114.0 | 66.0 | 113.0 | 293.0 |
| Movement | (15.5) | 21.3 | 32.8 | 38.6 |
| Overdraft/(balance) brought forward | 2.5 | (3.0) | 8.3 | 2.5 |
| Overdraft/(balance) carried forward | (13.0) | 8.3 | 41.1 | 41.1 |
| Overdraft facility to 30 September | 40.0 | 40.0 | 40.0 | 40.0 |

Figure 12    (Note: figures in brackets are positive)

must be available to meet day-to-day expenditure and by producing a cash flow forecast the builder should be able to arrange an overdraft with the bank in good time to prevent the company running out of cash. A sudden cash crisis suggests poor planning and may raise doubts in the bank manager's mind as to the soundness of the company. An example of a cash flow forecast is shown in Fig 12.

# 4
# DESIGN AND DEVELOPMENT

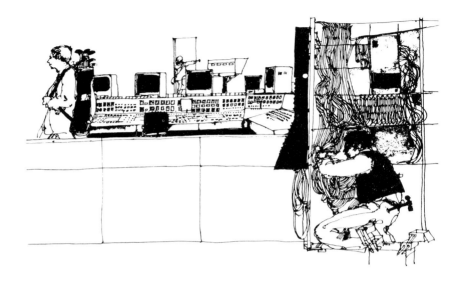

## Technology and Manufacturing Industry

The commercial world is highly competitive. Every enterprise must keep up with scientific and technological developments if it is to survive. In line with the speed of technical advance people's tastes are changing more quickly. Products of advanced design are in demand and will rapidly outsell traditional goods. Technical change often leads to reduced costs which in turn mean greater profitability.

In discussing technical innovation it is important to realise that every aspect of industry and commerce is involved. Manufacturing processes and production methods are affected as much as the product. In recent times technology has made a major contribution to the efficiency of business administration and management.

It is also necessary to remember that so-called 'high technology' is only a part of the overall contribution of the technologist to industry. Much that may appear to be ordinary has a large technical content.

The technologist cannot work in isolation from the other disciplines of commerce. He or she will be influenced by the market and the availability of funds. Industrial and human relations will have a pervasive influence and sometimes limit what is technically possible. Many technologists are required to be managers in their own right as well as technical experts.

## TECHNOLOGICAL ADVANCE

Technical progress is moving faster today than at any time in history, and the pace is still increasing. The silicon chip, in relative terms, is only at the beginning of its life and is already having a revolutionary effect.

New materials are replacing traditional ones or being used in a different way. For example, one reason why less steel is being used in the world is that, because of improvements to the specification, a given amount of steel can now be replaced by a much smaller amount which is just as strong. Similarly the introduction of the two-piece drinks can during the last ten years has meant the use of aluminium lids, paper-thin walls and engineering tolerances that are finer than those found in the average car engine.

Companies must constantly consider the use of new materials, otherwise their 'old-fashioned' lines will not stand up against better designed, cheaper or 'new look' products from their competitors.

New materials themselves may be less significant than the advantages they offer to the manufacturer. Plastic laundry baskets have no inherent advantage over old-fashioned wicker ones. They may even have a shorter life, be less attractive and use more expensive raw materials. However, they are cheap and can be made quickly in large quantities.

## MARKETING AND TECHNOLOGY

The technologist cannot work in isolation. Possible new products need to be critically examined for their marketing potential. In many instances the initiative for technological progress will come from the marketing department, whose analysis of market trends and customer needs may well identify new requirements without specifying how they are to be met. Marketing's task is to look ahead and devise products which will either satisfy developing public taste or take advantage of weak competition. Marketing will create technical problems for the company's designers and scientists to solve.

Sometimes technical departments discover processes and materials for which there is no immediate product application. Marketing's task then is to think up saleable applications. An example might be the special properties of irradiated plastic film which is now widely used to wrap frozen chickens.

Advances in micro-electronics have produced many new products in recent years and further product applications and refinements appear on the market almost daily. Each new product is designed to meet a need or to anticipate a demand. Pocket calculators have completely replaced the slide rule and in doing so have appealed to a far larger body of consumers. The same applies to the ubiquitous computer. Home computers are now commonplace and over half a million were bought as Christmas presents in 1983.

Technological advances which were developed for specialist use can be adapted for us all. Cameras, home movie equipment, watches, sun-glasses and many other products have benefited from such 'spin-off' advantages. Many consumer and industrial goods have developed as a result of the space race.

It is clear that the relationship between technology, marketing and commercial judgement is highly complex. It is mentioned here to show that technical matters cannot be isolated from other business activities.

## Product Development

As we have said, new product development is not an exercise for the scientist, engineer and technologist to conduct in isolation. There has to be a commercial justification for the development work. This might be to expand an existing market (say to sell more television sets). It could equally be to create new markets (TV games?) or to beat the competition, perhaps by developing TV sets with stereo sound. It is the combination of scientific investigation and market research that will provide the basic idea for a new or improved product. This idea must be refined into a specification from which detailed development work will flow.

This process is known as *product development*.

LIMITATIONS OF PRODUCT DEVELOPMENT

Matters for consideration in drawing up a development plan include: materials; production techniques; size of market; cost of development; production costs and pricing policy. Financial factors have an important influence on development planning.

The concept of product life was introduced in the previous chapter. Some items enjoy a very long product life while others last but a few years. The cost of development (together with the cost of setting up the production tools) has to be recovered by spreading that cost over a given production period. A long production run will enable the development cost per unit to be reduced.

If the market forecast indicates the likelihood of a short product life, then the cost of development will have to be recovered quickly

and each unit will need a high selling price. Even where the product
life is likely to be long, if the market is small the share of the development cost borne by each unit will have to be high.

The table below shows examples of how development costs can
affect a project. Product A will have a satisfactory life and will sell
well. Product B will not have such a long life but sales will be reasonable and the cost of each unit is still acceptable. Product C, like product A, has a good life but the market is small so that the share of the
development costs per unit are really too high.

|  | Product A | Product B | Product C |
|---|---|---|---|
| Development cost | £500,000 | £500,000 | £500,000 |
| Sales per year | 200,000 | 200,000 | 10,000 |
| Product life | 5 years | 2 years | 5 years |
| Total sales | 1,000,000 | 400,000 | 50,000 |
| Development cost per unit | £0.50 | £1.25 | £10 |
| Production cost per unit | £1 | £1 | £1 |
| Total cost per unit | £1.50 | £2.25 | £11 |

Figure 18

What would happen to each of the three products if the development cost was £1,500,000? At what stage does the product become
too expensive? These are the sort of policy questions that a company
must resolve before it decides to go ahead with a development
programme.

A real example of this type of difficulty would be the dilemma
facing some electronics manufacturers with regard to solid state TV.
This device would do away with the conventional tube and large
cabinet so that TV sets could be no thicker than a mirror and light
enough to hang on the wall. Such a product is technically feasible but
indications are that its appeal would be very limited. However, cus·
tomer attitudes might change quickly and the first manufacturer in
could both stimulate demand and clean up the market. Would you
go ahead?

SEQUENCE OF DEVELOPMENT

If the decision is to go ahead a development plan will be needed.
Fig 19 shows the main steps in the development of an idea to full production status.

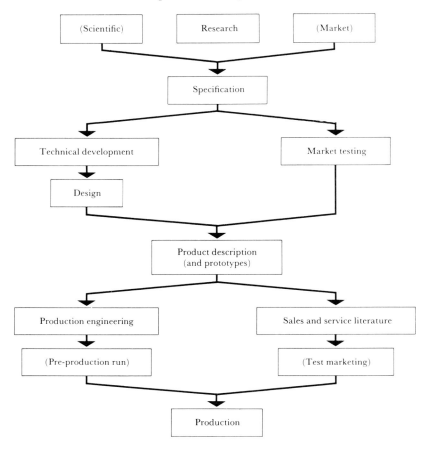

**Sequence of
product development**

Figure 19    Note how the technical activity is related to marketing

*Research*

In industry scientists either work in pure research (seeking new ideas and pursuing theories without any specific goal) or applied development (working towards a clearly defined objective).

The former is very costly and results cannot be guaranteed. As a result pure research is usually undertaken only in very large companies, in academic institutions, or with government sponsorship. Sometimes whole industries contribute towards a central research facility so that costs can be shared. For example, the Motor Industry Research Association provides expensive facilities that are shared by its members.

*Technical description (specification)*

The technical department must provide answers to the following questions concerning the product:

1 Design:
   Will the product work?
   Can it be made economically?
   Can it work more efficiently?
   What servicing will be required?
   How can it be made to look good?
   Is it safe?

2 Manufacturing methods:
   What is the best method of manufacture?
   What is the most economical method of manufacture?
   Where should it be made?
   Can fewer or different raw materials be used?

3 Quality control:
   Will it last?
   Does it conform to specification?
   Does it meet official standards?

The answers to these and many other questions will lead to the creation of a *technical description*. This document sets out what the product will do and how it will do it, the materials to be used, production methods and quality. However, at this stage the detailed design has not been produced and there is much research and testing still to be done. As part of the development programme a number of technical descriptions may have to be written.

*Technical development*

The development of the product from idea to saleable item is a matter of painstaking detail. Each aspect of the design must be checked. Can the product be assembled easily? When it is in service will maintenance be a problem? Acceptable quality levels must be established.

For example, the quality of a mechanical item will depend on how accurately the moving parts are made. The roughly made bearings suitable for a child's pedal toy would be totally unacceptable in an aircraft engine. High quality, accurately machined parts are expensive, but if this is what the customer requires and will pay for, then they will be included in the technical description.

Prototypes will be made and rigorously tested, both to ensure that the product works and that it will be acceptable to the customer. Mars Electronics have recently launched a radar for small boats and, over a period of two years, first'wooden mock-ups and then actual radar sets were taken down to the south coast to be critically viewed by weekend sailors.

In the case of consumer goods, such as a new supper dish or a re-formulated soap, a consumer test will be conducted. This may take the form of a test marketing exercise for which quite large-scale production is required. The extra cost of such an exercise is made worth while if it can be spread over a large number of sales (remember Fig 18).

## Production and Technology

The production process itself is highly technical and is described in the next chapter. The technical department of a company will, however, have a special contribution to make to the production process.

PRODUCT DESCRIPTIONS

The technical description led to the process of technical development. The result of the development work will be the *product description*. So far all the work on the new product has been in the hands of the technical department. Now this work can be passed on to the production department, and the product can be manufactured in bulk for sale to customers.

The production department needs to know all the details of the design; how it is to be made and put together, and also some idea of the size of the total task.

In reality this explanation of the sequence of events is over-simplified. We have already seen that the technical department had to consult with marketing and financial experts before it began its work. Similarly it will have been discussing production problems and methods with the production department long before issuing the product description.

The product description will include the following information:

1  Drawings of the product—both of the complete assembly and the component parts—giving all the dimensions and tolerances required to manufacture it.

2  A parts list giving details of all components, their material speci-

fications, the quantities required per product and whether the parts are made internally or 'bought in'. The parts list will also give details of all sub-assemblies that go to make up the final product.

3 Special customer requirements.

4 Test instructions. The responsibility of the technical department for quality control is looked at later. Test instructions—details of tests which must be carried out during production—are usually produced as part of the product description. These instructions will set out what the tests should be and the pass standard. There is often a safety consideration involved here and manufacturers of such products as electrical and gas fittings or pressure vessels have to attend to these matters very early in the development stage. Not to do so would be both illegal and dangerous, since products like these can cause real danger if they do not perform properly.

Fig 20 shows an assembly drawing for a household tap. Not perhaps the most technical item that we meet in our daily lives, but nonetheless the subject of considerable technical effort.

STANDARDISATION
A company's technical department can assist the production department in another way—namely standardisation. Technology is

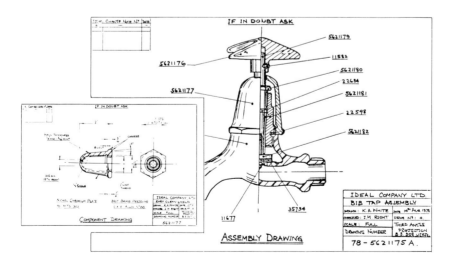

Figure 20

closely involved with mass production and efforts to speed the flow of goods. Mass production itself is based on extensive use of standard ways of working and (as we have seen) the use of specifications. Not surprisingly, therefore, certain products and materials are subject to standardisation agreements, which have semi-official, government or even international backing.

The British Standards Institution provides industry with the means of tackling national problems relating to standardisation and specifications. Standard safety features and dimensions exist for example for electrical goods, switches, building materials and the like.

Other examples of standardisation include domestic electrical fittings (plugs, bulbs, fuses etc) and items which call for a well-understood safety element. These are obvious areas where standardisation benefits industry and the community at large.

A very practical consideration is that costs can often be kept down if full advantage is taken of standard parts, fittings and quality. However, this can only be done if the original design is made with standardisation in mind and communication between departments is excellent.

Some enterprises manage to maintain a profitable spare-parts business by making sure that only spare parts manufactured by themselves will do the job. However, to provide a satisfactory level of service to customers this strategy relies on an efficient distribution system which can be costly. Whilst such an approach might benefit the maker of specialised plant and machinery, it would be of doubtful value in say the motor accessory business. It makes no sense for different companies to produce regularly needed components which are not interchangeable.

The technical director of a company must keep up to date with standards, ensure that the company's products conform to them and contribute to the setting of standards for the future.

TOOLING

Jigs, fixtures and press tools allow semi-skilled operators to produce a large volume of parts to the correct dimensions, without the operators having to exercise much skill—other than operating the machine correctly. Jigs either hold a product in the right place whilst it is being worked on or else they guide tools and punches to perform correctly. It is the tooling which is actually in contact with the machined item and which 'converts' it. Tools and punches wear out frequently and need constant maintenance.

The jig and tool designer is a highly skilled person but, increasingly, he or she is having to work with computer-aided equipment (see Chapter 5). Computerised (or *numerical*) control can give quicker and more accurate results than a human operator and even the most complex tasks are now being automated.

Toolmakers are responsible for manufacturing and maintaining the tools, jigs, fixtures and gauges required by the production department. They are highly skilled technicians who can produce the required tools to very fine limits. Sometimes they are guided by the production engineers and sometimes by the jig and tool designers. They might be responsible to either the production manager or to the technical manager.

INSPECTION AND QUALITY CONTROL

Even though production of the item may have started, the technical department is still involved; this time with *quality control*. Quality is checked by inspectors using gauges, micrometers and, where necessary, special test rigs. They normally report to a senior manager who is not part of the production team, eg the technical director or the managing director who has overall responsibility for quality.

Quality is tested and checked at all stages of production. In some cases every item is tested but this is not always necessary and many systems are based on random sampling and a series of mathematical tables (concerning probability) which have been developed from techniques used to check the quality of ammunition during World War II. The main inspection activities are:

1 Goods inward inspection. Materials required for production and bought-in components must be inspected on arrival at the factory to ensure that they are of the right quality. This activity is called *goods inward inspection* and is carried out before the items or materials are accepted for payment and before they are built into the company's products.
2 Inspecting work-in-progress. Having checked the materials to be used the inspection department now has overall responsibility for checking the work itself as it progresses, stage by stage.
3 Checking finished goods. Inspection at the completion stage ensures that products are meeting the company's standards. However, the whole question of quality is discussed further in Chapter 5.

## Computers

The development of micro-electronics in computers has brought about a revolution in the way data (information), calculations and numerical problems are handled. Vast amounts of information can now be processed very quickly, enabling business decisions to be taken in the light of many facts which could not previously have been assembled. Supermarkets now record daily the sales of each product and can check their stock levels almost at will. Already bank statements and records of money transfers show the very latest position and this can be equally true of company accounts (sales, purchases, debtors and creditors etc). It is theoretically possible for a hire-purchase company to find out the credit worthiness of would-be borrowers at the touch of a button.

Information processing is rapidly changing the nature of clerical work and office routines. Word processors (such as the one used to edit this book) are replacing typewriters almost as fast as these replaced the quill pen at the turn of the century. Copying machines are making carbon paper redundant and even taking over the function of printing machinery in some cases. Copies can be transmitted instantaneously from London to New York—reducing the need for air-mail.

The use of computers as a management tool is looked at in more detail in Chapter 7.

DEVELOPMENT

The capability of the latest computers is astonishing. Yet more exciting is the pace of development and the cheapness of the new technology. Compared with transportation, electronic data handling has made the equivalent of 6,000 years' progress from the wheel to Concorde in half a century. Ten times as much progress is expected in the next decade.

Almost before it reaches the market a new computer will be out of date. Similar other high technology items can be obsolete before they leave the design stage!

Just as size is being dramatically reduced so is cost. The equivalent of the pocket calculator (which would have been the size of a suitcase twenty years ago) is in real terms thirty times cheaper than when it was introduced.

CAD/CAM

These initials stand for *computer-aided design* and *computer-aided manu-*

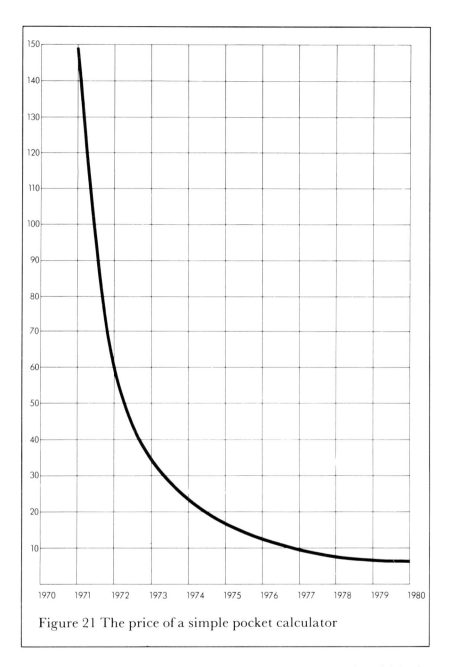

Figure 21 The price of a simple pocket calculator

*facturing.* They are important new areas for industry in which the power of the computer is used 'on screen' to increase productivity, not just for the production of drawings (CAD), but also for the extension of this basic data into related engineering fields (CAE).

Classic engineering activities, such as the best use of energy, stress and thermal properties, together with data connected with the normal manufacturing processes (CAM), can be linked together to work as one system. This is known as *computer-integrated manufacturing* (CIM).

The ultimate aim of all this is to integrate the three main manufacturing activities—design, engineering and production—so that they form one entity. Eventually the designers hope that the concept will develop to embrace such aspects of factory life as materials control, stock handling and, in due course, the supply of data into the company's financial computer system.

Two examples of possible uses of CIM may help to indicate the revolution such a system will bring. An engineer might obtain design information and then want to relate this to the cost of a drawing. Using the same terminal he or she will simply obtain access to the data on prices and choose the most cost-effective part or material for the job. From the same work station it will then be a straightforward operation to log into the word processing facility and prepare a specification.

In another example an electronics engineer might use an engineering work-station to complete a logic design and then pass the information through the communications network to another system. This done, another part of the operation will complete the layout of the PCB (printed circuit board) and the engineer can finish off, via the word processing facility, by writing a brief report.

At the heart of CIM lies the ability to transmit information from one facility to another, and from one department to another, and the opportunity not only to bring together engineering and manufacturing data, but to do so within the overall company information system. CIM is a good example of what is called information technology (it) which is itself a fast growing area.

TECHNOLOGY AND INDUSTRY

It is impossible to spell out all the implications of micro-electronics. New uses are being found daily, but one interesting change to the basic concepts of manufacturing has emerged. The complexity and smallness of silicon chips (and their associated circuitry) are making the manufacturing process a very delicate performance. The tiniest flaw in a component the size of a pinhead renders it both useless and irreparable. Where once the reject rate for mismade items would be acceptable at around 3 per cent, the movement away from mechanical methods of production to micro-electronic is making a lower rate

than this possible. Manufacturers of chips are looking for reject rates
of less than one in a million.

TECHNOLOGY AND SOCIETY
Many of the issues raised by advancing technology concern not just
industry but society itself. Technology may produce some social
problems (eg unemployment, acid rain and traffic jams) but, by the
same token, it also offers solutions, not only to these 'self-inflicted'
ills, but also to the age-old problems of mankind—disease, starvation and subsistence living conditions.

There are fears that computer information about individuals will
intrude on people's right to privacy. Individual tastes and personal
service could be lost as people are increasingly considered as mere
statistics. Products such as convenience foods, synthetic clothing
and pharmaceutical items not only change our individual lives but
can have a cumulative effect in altering the life-style of society.

It has been noted that industry seems to need progressively fewer
people to produce the nation's goods as our economy matures and
develops, and technology continues to advance. An increasing proportion of the working population finds employment in commerce,
government and service industries. Nevertheless, the type and
amount of employment created by industry is likely to continue to be
the prime influence on society's material standards. Unemployment
may be more a social than an industrial problem since, at its simplest
level, industry will continue to provide goods and thus create jobs—
if a buyer can be found. People without jobs, however, have limited
spending money and make poor buyers.

The influence of the new technology in social terms will be far-
reaching but it is probably wrong to jump to alarmist conclusions.
Fears of mass unemployment can perhaps be allayed by past experience. In 1830 250,000 men were employed in the British transport
industry. The building of the railways provided jobs for 2 million
men for twenty years and 250,000 men were needed to run the new
system; once the railway network was complete a similar number of
people (250,000) were required to provide local transport to and
from the railways!

In the census returns at the beginning of this century the largest
employment categories were domestic service and agriculture. The
former category is now so small it is not even shown on the latest
census forms, whilst agriculture currently employs only 2.7 per cent
of the work-force.

Thus we can see that changes in the social fabric brought about by technical innovation are not new, nor are they permanently damaging.

Technology will affect our life-style in a positive way, freeing people from monotonous jobs and offering more leisure time and the means to enjoy it. Again we have an example from the past. Air travel has severely reduced passenger sea traffic but more people now travel abroad, at cheaper fares and greater convenience. Employment generally in the international travel business has increased.

The day-to-day influence of technology on industry is less dramatic than may be supposed. Well-established technical skills have a vital role and new products are as much the result of pains-taking attention to detail and teamwork as they are of exciting new discoveries.

# 5
# PRODUCTION

### What is Production?

It may appear that without a product to make and sell a company cannot have a production department. However, some companies do not make things, but provide a service (eg a decorating company). Somebody in such a business has to plan and organise the work to ensure that it is undertaken to the satisfaction of customers. In this sense these people are the service industry's equivalent of the production function. They provide the product. However, it is easier to grasp concepts which embrace tangible items therefore the production function studied here is typical of a manufacturing company.

The approach a company adopts to establish its product range and its markets has already been explained. Making the goods may not be a matter of making every item from basic raw materials—in fact it very rarely is. For the most part manufacturers start with materials that have already been prepared in some way. Car-makers for instance use steel sheet for the basic structure of the car; they get the sheet from steel-makers and not from their own foundry.

SOURCES OF COMPONENTS

The first step in setting up a production process is therefore to decide how much of the fashioning of materials will be done by the company. What components will be purchased from outside, and what will be made in-house? This exercise will help to determine the resources required to achieve the manufacturing aims. By *manufacturing resources* we mean buildings, labour, materials, machines, equipment, tools and know-how.

### Buying in

Very few companies manufacture all the components for their product. It is cheaper and easier to buy specialist parts from a specialist manufacturer. A good example would be the metal hinges used in some furniture. Such components are said to be *bought-in*.

### Factoring

Extending the idea of buying in parts, it is quite common for companies to buy complete products from other companies and resell them as their own! These are called *factored* goods and require no in-house production work, other than inspection, to see they meet the specification. Factored goods can be used to complete a company's range of products without it having to provide small-volume items or to do things it is not good at.

Take for example a saucepan manufacturer. The pans might be made from aluminium castings produced in the company's foundry and finished off in the machine shop. Many people like to have a set of matching saucepans and a useful accessory is a steamer. This sits on a pan of boiling water to cook fish or vegetables or to reheat pre-cooked dishes. Steamers are not made from aluminium but by pressing out metal sheet. Our company has no machinery or experience for this work and won't sell enough steamers to make setting up a new department worth while. To complete its range of saucepans with the right accessories it therefore buys in complete steamers, finished in its own range of colours. The customer is encouraged to buy the company's pans because everything can now be matched.

### Production planning

Plans for buying in and factoring are an important part of the production process. Specifications must be checked to see that parts will fit together and suppliers must be well briefed on quantity, quality and delivery schedules.

Having decided which products and components are going to be made internally the manufacturer can then work out what resources are required. This exercise has to be undertaken in great detail.

## Manufacturing Resources

Apart from money (see Chapter 2) the main resources used by a manufacturing company are:

1  Land and buildings.
2  People.
3  Materials.
4  Machines and equipment.
5  Tools.

Service industries will share some of these needs, certainly buildings, personnel and machinery—in this case office equipment, such as typewriters.

In discussing the manufacturing requirements each aspect will be considered as if a new venture was being started. In reality the majority of new products are made by companies to replace an old line of manufacture. When starting a new line companies always have to recognise what resources, in terms of existing buildings, machinery and skills etc, they already have. Sometimes these items will prevent the product being produced in the ideal way, but this may have to be. If a totally novel item is envisaged it may be cheaper to start another company and use a 'green-field' site.

LAND AND BUILDINGS

One of the first considerations is what size and type of buildings are required to cope with the production operation and the volumes required. The design and shape of a building is very important and for that reason many factories are purpose-built. If the roof is too high then heating costs will be excessive. If the doors are too small and badly positioned then handling of materials and goods will cost more than necessary.

Enough space for the job is needed. If possible it should be sufficient to allow the various operations and processes to be laid out in a logical sequence. Too much space will cost the company excessive rent and rates; however, some space should be readily available for future expansion. Too little space will not allow sufficient room for the storage of goods and products between operations (ie work-in-progress) and this will lead to bottle-necks, which will slow down production and increase manufacturing time. This could make the company less efficient than its competitors.

Besides buildings, a company requires additional land for storing materials, holding finished goods, providing access for lorries and parking employees' cars. New building projects have to provide a statutory number of car-park spaces according to the floor area and the purpose for which the building is to be used. Planning permission will almost certainly be refused if this requirement is not met.

## PEOPLE

It is necessary to calculate how many operators (*direct workers*) and how many service workers (*indirects*) are required to achieve the manufacturing plan. Service workers will include those who maintain the machinery, clerks, drivers, cleaners, supervisors etc. Although they are referred to as 'indirect', these people are still essential to the job in hand. The direct workers include some people who are not actually operating machinery, like working charge hands and inspectors.

The number of people that are needed can be discovered once the plan for making the product has been settled. This plan is called a *process planning layout*. It shows each operation and movement as well as giving production times—from which the number of people and types of skills required can be calculated.

These numbers will be worked out in line with the time per operation and the quantities required per day.

Indirect labour in the factory will be calculated with the intention of providing sufficient back-up service to support the direct operators who actually manufacture products. The number of managers and supervisors will for instance depend on the complexity of the operations and the number of direct and indirect operatives to be supervised.

Arrangements must be made for training the labour force in the operation of new machines and processes. This exercise could involve assistance from outside sources and must take place before production is scheduled to start.

## MATERIALS

The purchasing department will have to work out the amount of raw materials and components that will be needed and these must be ordered from suppliers. To allow for the suppliers' delivery time (or *lead time*) and to insure against any delay, companies normally maintain some form of stock-holding and try to obtain at least two approved suppliers for each item if possible. However, stocks cost money; so they have to be controlled and a delicate balance must be maintained between tying up too much money and running out of raw materials.

MACHINES AND EQUIPMENT

If production is to be efficient, the appropriate machines must be used. The selection of this machinery and the design of jigs and fixtures is the job of the production engineer. Close liaison between the design department and the production engineering department is necessary to ensure that the most economic methods of production are used.

Having determined the best mix of tools and machines the production engineer is then faced with the problem of laying out the production area. This layout might take the form of a sequential flow of activities (ie a production line) or a grouping of machines so that work can be done in batches. The various methods have their advantages and are discussed a little further on page 82.

The machinery and equipment which is installed could be standard items that can be purchased easily. Sometimes, however, the need is for special-purpose machines designed specifically for the job. In this case orders must be given to the machine-makers in good time or production will be held up until they are delivered. The lead time for such items can often be as long as six months to a year.

Some machinery is very expensive indeed and could add too much to the cost of setting up production (and therefore to the selling price). Companies will normally keep the number of expensive machines to a minimum, but try to make the best use of any they do buy by working them as long as possible. People only work for part of each day—usually eight hours. Theoretically this means that the machinery they use will be idle for sixteen hours each day, or two-thirds of its life. A second and even third set of operators can be introduced to work the machines when they would otherwise have been sitting unused. This is called *shift working*.

Shift work designed to make best use of machinery should not be confused with continuous production schedules which are made necessary by the nature of the process itself. Glass, bricks and steel manufacture cannot be started in the span of a normal working day and have to be kept going by twenty-four-hour shift work.

Another example of process production is the Maxwell House spray-dry coffee plant at Banbury. These huge machines are made entirely of stainless steel and turn the coffee beans into the familiar instant coffee. They are run virtually all year round, twenty-four hours a day, and to cope with this the factory has had as many as eight different shift patterns.

TOOLS
The tools, which may be either jigs holding the part whilst a hole is drilled in the right position, or press tools piercing and forming sheet metal, are manufactured by toolmakers. If the company has a constant demand for tool manufacture and repair it may pay to employ its own highly skilled toolmakers. The tooling required is decided at the process-planning stage by the production engineer. He or she will consider the type of machines being used as well as the type and ability of the operators.

For example, if large batches of a standard product are required, the individual manufacturing operations can be 'de-skilled' by producing tools that semi-skilled operators can use easily and accurately.

## Manufacturing Instructions

There are three basic ways of setting about making things:

1 Very special items are made as *one-off* 'jobs'. An example might be the sort of special tool that was mentioned in the preceding paragraphs.
2 When several units are needed they can be produced in *batches*.
3 Continuous flow *processes* are used for the mass production of goods that are required in bulk. Many everyday things are made in this way—felt pens, soap powder and pocket calculators for example. Continuous flow methods are also used in the production of goods for industry, eg cement works, oil refineries and the production of steel.

These different methods of production have their own particular characteristics and working environment. Each has a different affect on the size of the factory, number of employees, control methods, demands on workers, and the type of management style. Above all there is a sharp contrast in the physical conditions found within each type of production method and the attitudes required to make them work well.

Once the method of production has been set up—and this is largely determined by the type of product—the production manager's role is to *schedule* and *control* the work. This is a daily task carried out against a constantly changing background.

The start point is an overall plan which shows the quantities of each product to be made and the date they are required. This information comes from the sales forecast.

The next step is a detailed *work schedule* for each item and this explains the task of each department within the production function and its part in the whole operation. It is made out by the production manager's staff, who must personally supervise the work and take corrective action if delays arise. A variety of different departments help in this control activity and the role each has to play will be explained in later sections.

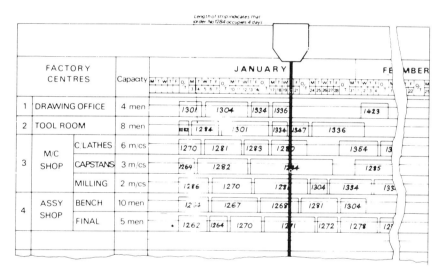

Figure 22 Work schedule Orders are entered on the loading board according to the time they occupy the full capacity of each factory centre. Thus, if an order requires 16 man days of drawing office time and there are four draughtsmen, this will be entered as 4 days.

---

## Production Services

A manufacturing company requires production services, ie departments which make a contribution to the production process, without being directly involved in it. They are:

1  Production drawing office.
2  Production engineering.
3  Work study (or industrial engineering).
4  Production control.
5  Inspection and quality control.
6  Maintenance.
  7  Purchasing.


These services will normally be under the control of the production manager. Others that are equally important may be under someone else's control. In Chapter 4, on technology, we noted that quality control is usually independent of the production department. Other functions that can operate in this way include the buying of supplies, jig design and toolmaking.


PRODUCTION DRAWING OFFICE

Once a product has been designed and tested to ensure that it works properly, it is necessary to produce manufacturing drawings. In some companies these manufacturing drawings are produced in a section of the design office. In others there is a separate production drawing office. The drawings produced are specifically for the production and factory staff and are not seen by customers. Each component of the product must be drawn to show all the detail of its design. Dimensions always show machining tolerances, and sometimes surface finishes, thread dimensions, heat treatment requirements and plating specifications are included. The production drawing office staff work closely with other people in the production area to ensure that the goods can be produced as economically as possible.

At the moment a revolution is taking place in the drawing office through the use of computer-aided design (CAD). This allows staff to produce drawings much more quickly and to adopt a more sophisticated approach. For example, some CAD systems allow the operator to look at the design from another angle or to include drawings of previously entered components, just by pressing a button. (For further information refer back to Chapter 4).


PRODUCTION ENGINEERING

The production engineers work very closely with the drawing office staff to ensure that the design makes it as easy as possible for the products to be made properly. It is relatively straightforward to make a prototype in the research centre but a great technical challenge lies in making the leap from laboratory bench to factory floor. Will the product still be properly made by tired operatives on the night shift in another plant three years from now?

Production engineers play a key part in this 'scaling-up' process, not only foreseeing problems but solving them before they occur. Time and material which is wasted on the production line while 'teething problems' are sorted out is very expensive.

Production engineers operate in many manufacturing locations. Not only will they be found in the more obvious places such as the car, aerospace and machine-tool industries, they are also needed in food processing as well as pharmaceutical, glass and plastics production.

Like their counterparts in the drawing office they are also being affected by new technology in the form of CAE (computer-aided engineering), but for more about this see Chapter 4.

We have seen that product descriptions, drawings and specifications come from the design drawing office. On their own these are not always sufficient to allow the products to be made, because unless the operators are skilled they may not be able to read technical drawings. Therefore *manufacturing instructions* which can be clearly understood in the factory must be produced. These are called *process planning layouts* and are prepared by production engineers.

These give written details of how each component, sub-assembly and final assembly should be produced. They give the sequence of operations, the machines to be used, their speeds and the time each operation should take. In particular they will attempt to dovetail the various operations so that everything fits together. If several thousand components are used in making a car then the complexity of this activity is obvious.

Each operator has access to copies of the process planning layouts and by reading the instructions in conjunction with the appropriate drawings he or she is able to produce the component or assembly correctly. In some industries, eg electronics, photographs are also used to supplement drawings of intricate assembly operations since they can provide a clearer illustration of what has to be achieved.

To check that all the preparation is complete many factories carry out 'pre-production runs', staffed by production engineers and specially selected workers. Once the tooling has been proven and the products manufactured in the required quantities to the right quality, the job is handed over to the supervisors who are responsible

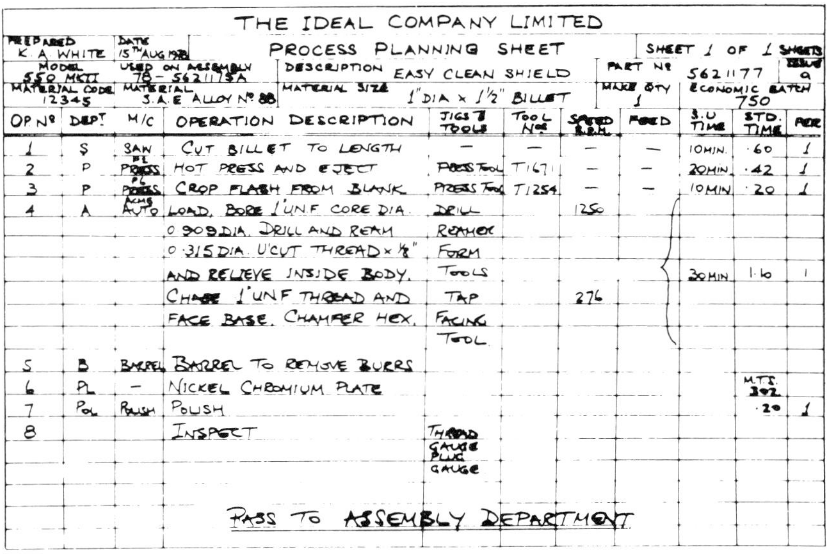

THE IDEAL COMPANY LIMITED

PROCESS PLANNING SHEET

PREPARED: K. A. WHITE | DATE: 15TH AUG 1983 | SHEET 1 OF 1 SHEETS

MODEL: 550 MKII | USED ON ASSEMBLY: 78 - 5621175A | DESCRIPTION: EASY CLEAN SHIELD | PART No: 5621177 | ISSUE: a

MATERIAL CODE: 12345 | MATERIAL: S.A.E. ALLOY No 88 | MATERIAL SIZE: 1" DIA × 1½" BILLET | MAKE QTY: 1 | ECONOMIC BATCH: 750

| OP No | DEPT | M/C | OPERATION DESCRIPTION | JIGS & TOOLS | TOOL Nos | SPEED R.P.M. | FEED | S.U TIME | STD. TIME | PER |
|---|---|---|---|---|---|---|---|---|---|---|
| 1 | S | SAW | CUT BILLET TO LENGTH | — | — | — | — | 10MIN. | ·60 | 1 |
| 2 | P | PL PRESS | HOT PRESS AND EJECT | PRESS TOOL | T1671 | — | — | 20MIN. | ·42 | 1 |
| 3 | P | PC PRESS | CROP FLASH FROM BLANK | PRESS TOOL | T1254 | — | — | 10MIN | ·20 | 1 |
| 4 | A | ACME AUTO | LOAD. BORE 1"UNF CORE DIA. | DRILL | | 1250 | | | | |
| | | | 0·909 DIA. DRILL AND REAM | REAMER | | | | | | |
| | | | 0·315 DIA. U'CUT THREAD × ⅛" | FORM | | | | | | |
| | | | AND RELIEVE INSIDE BODY. | TOOLS | | | | 30MIN | 1·16 | 1 |
| | | | CHASE 1"UNF THREAD AND | TAP | | 276 | | | | |
| | | | FACE BASE. CHAMFER HEX. | FACING | | | | | | |
| | | | | TOOL | | | | | | |
| 5 | B | BARREL | BARREL TO REMOVE BURRS | | | | | | | |
| 6 | PL | — | NICKEL CHROMIUM PLATE | | | | | | M.T.S. 302 | |
| 7 | POL | POLISH | POLISH | | | | | | ·20 | 1 |
| 8 | | | INSPECT | THREAD GAUGE PLUG GAUGE | | | | | | |

PASS TO ASSEMBLY DEPARTMENT

Figure 23 Process planning layout

for day-to-day manufacture. Thereafter, the production engineer becomes a 'trouble-shooter' responsible for resolving any production problems that may occur in the future.

WORK STUDY

This activity is concerned with using the work-force (both direct and indirect labour) to best effect. Once production is under way and the operators have become reasonably experienced at their jobs, the work study engineer can start to find ways to produce the product and its components even more efficiently—which normally means in less time. This is done by examining the flow of work and the way in which it is carried out.

Results are obtained by painstaking attention to detail. To start with each activity is carefully timed. This will be done on many occasions and at different periods of the day, because people cannot work at the same pace all the time. Schedules which are based on one observation might be impossible to maintain or they could be hopelessly slow! Allowances must be made for rest, meal breaks and the natural variation in speed of work that happens during the day.

Work study is a relatively new science and, in its early stages, it was very unpopular with operators who saw it as an attempt to set fast working speeds that would make life a constant race against the clock. In fact the work study engineer is anxious to make the job of the operator easier. Time is but one factor in work evaluation and is mostly used as a guide, to measure the effect of the overall plan and the present levels of efficiency.

Much can be achieved by studying the layout of machines and the sequence of events. Reaching for inaccessible controls, lifting heavy parts unnecessarily and struggling with poorly marked dials can make the operator's life difficult. Improvements will lead to greater speed of work and at the same time make the job less tiring.

Operating times are used for planning the workload, for measuring the efficiency of the operator against the standard, and also as a basis for bonus or incentive schemes. These reward operators financially for working more efficiently.

PRODUCTION CONTROL

The primary task of the production control department is to develop the sales plan into the production or manufacturing plan. For example, the sales department might require 200 units of a particular product per month and it may take a day to organise the making of a batch plus two days to complete the 200 units. Because the setting up time for 400 units and 200 units will be the same it may be better to produce 400 units on each run and only manufacture six times a year.

There is not always an easy solution to such problems. In this case, for instance, there might not be enough storage space to hold the extra 200 units for a whole month.

The task is to use production facilities and labour effectively and to balance economic batch sizes with customer demand. At the same time the controllers must ensure that stocks are kept at economic and sensible levels.

Thus the production control department is the 'nerve centre' of a manufacturing company. Amongst its detailed responsibilities are:

1  Planning, monitoring and controlling the factory workload so that sales requirements are met. It has to do this in such a way that the shop-floor operates efficiently, customers get their goods when they want them and everyone knows clearly what is wanted and by when.
2  Issuing the documents which tell the factory what to produce, how many and when. This is known as the production programme.
3  Informing the works management if the production programme is

falling behind and suggesting corrective action to bring it back on plan.

4 Liaising with the marketing department so that the forward load of orders is neither too great or too small for the factory. Needless to say matching capacity to orders is an almost impossible task.

In short the task of the production control function is to try to ensure the maximum utilisation of all manufacturing resources. It will aim to do this by co-ordinating the activities of the sales department, drawing office, buying, stock control, production engineering, work study, manufacturing and accounts.

INSPECTION

Responsibility for the inspection of production work should always be divorced from the production department. Quality control is therefore usually exercised by the technical department, as previously mentioned, who should be responsible to either the works director or the board of directors. Their job is to ensure that faultless construction, good design, reliable bought-in components and clear operating methods add up to 'fitness for purpose'. If these factors exist they will enable the company to sell products that give value for money.

The inspection department's verdict is the acid test for the whole manufacturing operation.

This not to say that members of the production team themselves have no responsibility for the inspection of their work. Allowance for this must be made in the process planning layout, otherwise delays will be caused. Indeed the best and latest quality control systems are based on workers being made responsible for the quality of their own work and for that of their fellow workers.

At Jaguar Cars the philosophy has changed from one of inspecting out faults to one of building in quality. Jaguar believe that the 50 per cent sales growth achieved by them in the USA during 1981 was directly attributable to improved quality.

MAINTENANCE

The maintenance department is another engineering service department. Its job is to ensure that machines and equipment are kept in full working order and its responsibilities may also include the repair of buildings. To this end it may call on outside specialists, eg roofing experts and boiler service contractors. This department often works on a shift basis, carrying out its repairs when the plant and equipment is not in full use. Wherever possible preventive maintenance is carried out before machines break down. This means replacing a part that has a twelve-month life cycle in eleven months. Many factories operate a preventive maintenance schedule.

Continuous processes which work round the clock present special problems for the maintenance team. The solution is to shut down the plant at set intervals and carry out a complete check—replacing parts that are near the end of their life. The interval between shutdowns is critical—too long and plant failure will cause disruption, and even danger; too short and time and money are wasted. Experience is the only sure guide to the right answer.

PURCHASING

Supplies of materials, machines and bought-in parts are vital to a company. The quantities needed will probably be very large and mistakes will be expensive. The people who do the buying must have a specialist knowledge of what is available and at what price. They must be able to evaluate potential suppliers. Is their quality control good? Can they deliver on time? Will they keep up with developments and provide the very latest goods? Are they reliable? These are some of the questions that buyers must answer, and finding the answers is not always easy.

There are four main areas of concern:

1 Quality.
2 Delivery.
3 Price.
4 Reliability.

Very often price, although very important, is not the key requirement. Consistently good quality is the vital attribute which the purchasing function will be seeking in a potential supplier. This and a reliable delivery service are far more important than a few pence less in price. The reason is fairly obvious. In any factory, time is money because stocks are waiting to be used, wages are clocking up, machines are running and customers are waiting. In this type of situation a reject load of components or raw materials from an outside supplier can bring the factory to a halt.

Equally as bad as this is the type of quality problem which either slows down the manufacturing operation or is not detected until a large number of finished goods have been made. Steel sheet which has minute pin holes in it means a lot of reject Coke cans.

Thus the people working in purchasing have to make sure that the company is:

1 Getting the best value for money.
2 Always holding the right stock.
3 Managing its stores and warehouses efficiently.

This requires constant communication with other people, both within the company and in those businesses which are supplying goods and services. New suppliers and new products must be investigated. In many companies the value of orders placed by the purchasing department accounts for 60 per cent or more of the total production cost.

## Control

The important thing to remember is that nothing on the manufacturing floor is random. What goes on is based on plans that have been put together days and weeks in advance.

It is pointless preparing plans unless some form of monitoring takes place to ensure that they are being met. Controls are the means by which a record of actual performance is kept on a regular basis. Results can then be compared with the plan, with the differences being shown as *variances*, positive or negative as the case may be.

Variances need to be looked at overall. For example, a company may produce 1,000 less than planned of a certain product in a week, but cumulatively for the month the results may show that production is 2,000 ahead of target, even after taking into account the one-week shortfall.

An efficient manufacturing company will have controls that cover the main areas of activity. For example, apart from budgetary control exercised by the accountant, controls will almost certainly be in use in the following areas:

1 Orders.
2 Production.
3 Stock.
4 Labour cost.

The control systems must provide a means of highlighting problems in time to adjust plans accordingly. If adverse trends are not detected soon enough for action to be taken, then it is pointless producing control information. It will only confirm that the damage has been done and it is too late to do anything.

ORDER CONTROL

The production department must know how sales are going and what orders have been secured. Otherwise there will be overproduction of some items and panics to provide more of others. Given advance warning of the trends, action can be taken to divert resources to the production of goods that are proving popular, and vice versa.

Getting information in good time is vital. Production depends on materials and parts that are supplied from other companies. They in turn will have planned their production and will not be able to double or halve deliveries suddenly. Similarly changes in the rate of production may affect the number of workers needed. Operators cannot be found and trained overnight.

Order control is designed to ensure that the workload of the factory is maintained as evenly as possible throughout the year. It is a difficult task. However providing the control system keeps managers informed of the up-to-date situation either daily, weekly or monthly, they will be able to take appropriate action.

PRODUCTION CONTROL

The information produced by the production control department translates the workload into time. The time it will take to produce what is needed depends on the capacity of the machines and people available.

When the production programme has been compiled it must be cleared with the management and supervision responsible for production.

Control is exercised by comparing the results achieved by each department with the targets each one was set. The information needed to do this can be acquired in many ways. One method is to issue a *batch document*. Attached to it are *job cards* for each operation, and as each task is completed the job card is torn off and returned to production control who can thus monitor progress.

Having noted any variance from the planned programme the production control department informs the appropriate supervisor of the action he or she must take to get output back on programme, eg in the case of a bottle-neck to work overtime on a particular section.

## STOCK CONTROL

Stock control is closely connected with production control. The right materials, components and bought-in parts must be available when required or there can be no production. We have seen that the amount of stock that a company holds can be expensive and it is vital that stocks of the finished product are tightly controlled. Stocks have to be bought and paid for and if the stores are too full money is being wasted. The stock control system will be based on policy decisions made by the board of directors regarding the amount of stock the company should hold and the level of customer service the company intends to offer.

The stock control system is often run by the purchasing department, in conjunction with the warehouse, and works by telling the buyers when stocks of materials and bought-in parts should be re-ordered.

## LABOUR COST CONTROL

Labour cost controls keep management informed of the output achieved by and the cost of the labour force. Targets, which are set with the help of work study, are compared with the time actually spent by the operators in carrying out the work. Managers and supervisors use these controls as a guide to the efficiency of each department and when adverse trends are shown they can take the necessary corrective action.

## WAREHOUSE

In some manufacturing companies the warehouse (where raw materials and finished goods are stored awaiting delivery to either the factory or the customer) is the responsibility of the production department. In others it is the responsibility of sales or marketing. The warehouse is the final stage in the production process.

The warehouse manager or supervisor is not only required to store valuable finished goods efficiently, but also to plan delivery schedules so that customers get their goods on time. Efficient use of all the means of distribution available (ie company vehicles, sub-contract lorries, carriers, British Rail etc) will also be a warehouse responsibility. The warehouse has to marshal goods in the correct order sequence to allow vehicles to be loaded and despatched quickly.

# 6
# PEOPLE AT WORK

## Introduction

At the very beginning of this book we laid great stress on the fact that industry is about people. Now we shall consider those people. In previous chapters we have seen what they do and how their different skills are used in the many departments of a company. What do they get in return?

The obvious answer is 'money', and this is true. The people employed in industry are paid for their labours, but there is more to their contract than work and cash. There is the question of job satisfaction. People like to do a good job. To do this they need the right conditions, tools and training. They like to know that their efforts are appreciated and they are contributing something. These extra elements of the reward for work are influenced by the personal relationships between individuals. In this chapter we will examine some of the ways in which these relationships work.

STRIFE?

The news media are apt to dwell on the less satisfactory aspects of the relationships between managers and managed. It cannot be denied that trade unions and management represent different, if not opposing, interests. Yet for the most part the two 'sides' of industry work in greater harmony than might be supposed from reading newspapers.

Time lost in industry through strikes is less than that lost through sickness or absenteeism. The worst year for working days lost as a result of disputes during the past few years was 1979 when 29 million working days were lost. The latest figures for sickness absence show that last year 358 million working days were recorded as lost. However, the figure is more like 600 million if people who are off sick for less than three days are included. Our strike record is by no means the worst in the Common Market and in 1982 only 5 million days were lost through stoppages.

We each have a personal opinion on the issues of the day, but too often the heat of argument blinds us to the underlying facts. The role of trade unions and the rights and duties of employees and the organisations for which they work are recognised as vital questions in today's debate about how our society works. Not surprisingly, this debate is highly political, but in the context of daily work the ideological and partisan differences between individuals are rarely significant.

PERSONAL RELATIONSHIPS

At an individual level human relations in industry are no different from those found in society at large. We all know people whom we dislike just as we all have friends. However carefully the relationships within industry are analysed, the essentially personal nature of the relationship between individual managers and their staff, between managers themselves, and between managers and other members of the company, must not be forgotten.

## Managing People

All companies, whether large or small, need the function of personnel management. Larger companies usually employ specialist personnel managers to do this work. In smaller companies line managers may well be responsible for personnel matters in addition to their other tasks. A line manager is someone who is directly involved in providing the company's products; production, technical control, sales and distribution are the 'line' functions. They are also referred to as 'operational' roles. Personnel managers, like accountants, provide specialist advice and help to the line managers.

The Institute of Personnel Management provides the following definition:

Personnel management is a responsibility of all those who manage people, as well as being a description of the work of all those who are employed as specialists. It is that part of management which is concerned with people at work and with the relationships within an enterprise. It applies not only to industry but to all fields of employment.

Personnel management aims to achieve both efficiency and justice, neither of which can be pursued successfully without the other. It seeks to bring together and develop into an effective organisation men and women who make up an enterprise, enabling each to make their own best contribution to its success, both as individuals and as members of the work group. It seeks to provide fair terms and conditions of employment and satisfying work for those employed.

Whether or not there is a specialist personnel manager every manager in industry has a part to play in the management of people. The personnel manager provides a specialist service to management, but this service does not reduce the responsibility of each individual manager to establish a good relationship with his or her staff; it seeks to strengthen such relationships.

RESPONSIBILITIES

Although a company may have a personnel manager, this does not reduce the line managers' responsibility for the day-to-day well-being of employees under their control or the quality of their work. There is a danger that the line managers may take charge of 'things' and leave the personnel department to look after the people. This is never satisfactory.

There are, however, matters which should not be determined by individual managers on their own. These are items which are better handled within a policy for the company as a whole. Pay and terms of service come into this category. Similarly line managers will not have the necessary expertise to ensure that the company complies with its many legal obligations towards employees. All these items are tasks for the personnel department.

In summary the job of the personnel manager includes most of the following:

1 Advising management on employment law.
2 Recruiting.

3  Training, assessment, promotion and career development.
4  Keeping employment records.
5  Advising on conditions of service.
6  Controlling wage, salary and pension administration.
7  Staff benefits and welfare facilities.
8  Negotiating with trade unions.

EMPLOYMENT LAW
Employees are protected by a score of major Acts of Parliament and many minor ones. The main protections and privileges afforded to any person taking a job include:

 1  Non-discrimination on grounds of sex and race.
 2  Freedom to join a trade union.
 3  Provision of safe and healthy working conditions.
 4  Protection from arbitrary or unjustified dismissal.
 5  Contractual obligations by companies to pay agreed rates of pay
    for agreed hours.
 6  Protection for young persons against exploitation.
 7  Pension provision.
 8  Paid holidays.
 9  Redundancy payment.
10  Maternity benefits.
11  Compensation for accidents at work.

Much of the legal framework covering employment is of recent origin, and companies have had to absorb it rapidly. As so often happens, the law has largely enforced what was already established practice in forward-looking companies, and compelled others to follow suit. As employees we may feel fully entitled to the rights the law gives us, but we must also recognise that only the underlying prosperity of an organisation can provide the guarantee of secure employment.

RECRUITING
An efficient recruitment procedure is essential for a modern, well-run company. The preparation of advertisements, checking applications and selecting applicants for interview takes time. Interviewing requires special skills. References must be checked and proper employment agreements prepared. The 'mechanics' of recruiting are almost always left to the personnel department, although line

managers will usually make the final choice of candidate from a short list of two or three.

## TRAINING

At a conservative estimate, half the jobs which exist in industry today did not exist in their present form twenty years ago. Many companies are operating in industries which did not then exist. We can expect more changes in the future and people entering industry today may have to retrain and acquire new skills at least once, and possibly twice, during their working life.

Industry understands the need for organised training, but during the recession many organisations have found it hard to fund what was needed. Not surprisingly, larger companies tend to do more training per employee since they are able to devote more resources to employee development.

To try to ensure a consistent standard of training the government set up a number of *Industry Training Boards,* each dealing with one specialised sector of industry (eg the Hotel and Catering Industry Training Board). However, early in the eighties these were cut back and there are now only seven.

In parallel with the efforts of the government to improve training, various learned bodies establish standards in particular skills. The professional institutions are best known in this respect, many being extremely old. In most instances it is not possible to practise a profession without the relevant qualification, and this limitation is often taken as the distinction of a true 'profession'.

The training function in industry tackles a wide range of programmes which include:

1 Induction.
2 Safety.
3 Personal skills.
4 Collective training.
5 Development of individual potential.
6 Retraining for new skills and technology.

## CONDITIONS OF EMPLOYMENT

Every employee must know the terms on which he or she is employed. In fact these conditions form a contract of employment and include:

1 Hours of work.
2 Pay.

3  Holidays.
4  Responsibilities.
5  Privileges.
6  Sick leave provisions.
7  Discipline and grievance procedures.

PAY

The conflict which exists between the employee's need to earn a living and the company's need to survive and prosper is a real one. It exists in all organisations from small private companies to the nationalised industries and multi-national giants.

Companies must manage two distinct aspects of paying their employees. First, they must control the size of their pay-roll in relation to other costs and the amount coming in from sales. Secondly they must satisfy and reconcile individual or collective pressures for more pay. The relative earnings of individuals or groups of employees should be acceptable both to the management of the company and to the employees concerned. In the large company particularly, the personnel manager will have to cope with the difficult problem of pay differentials—not just 'how much' but 'how much in relation to the other person'.

WELFARE

As well as meeting these legal obligations an employer will wish to provide the best working conditions that can be afforded. Some amenities will be of a general nature (eg sports facilities), while others represent a measurable benefit to individual employees. Luncheon Vouchers, subsidised canteens and free protective clothes are examples.

Another category of benefits is aimed at improving pay scales. In many instances the growth of benefits has reflected a desire to avoid high levels of personal taxation (a motive that may or may not be socially acceptable). Contrary to popular belief such benefits are not always restricted to the more senior managers, but are frequently available to all employees (eg discount schemes for the purchase of company products and miners' free coal).

From time to time we all have problems of a personal nature which will prey on our minds and affect our work. The good employer or manager will wish to help, both out of personal sympathy, and for the practical necessity of maintaining efficiency. Frequently the personnel manager will be involved but, in a well-run company, the line managers will demonstrate their leadership qualities by concerning themselves with the welfare of their subordinates.

NEGOTIATING WITH TRADE UNIONS
Normally it is the task of the personnel manager to represent the company during negotiations with the trade unions.

As this involves putting the management point of view accurately it can only be done if the manager concerned has the support and confidence of the board of directors. He or she will certainly have made a careful study of negotiating techniques.

## Trade Unions

HISTORY
The coming together of workers to apply pressure on their employers, usually with the aim of improving wages or conditions of work, has a long history. The present-day trade unions have their origins in the first half of the nineteenth century when increasingly successful attempts were made to organise workers. Step by step the law came to recognise the legitimacy of workers' organisations and their activities, but the struggle was not without physical confrontation and personal sacrifice.

During the first sixty years of the last century, there was a continual ebb and flow in the strength of trade unionism. In 1868, however, the movement could be said to have achieved adulthood when the first Trades Union Congress (TUC) was held. The union movement consolidated as the scale of industrialisation grew in Victorian Britain. Full legal recognition of trade unions did not come until the 1920s; membership continued to grow until it reached a peak of just over 13 million in 1979.

TYPES OF UNION
Trade unions are independent associations of groups of working people. Historically there are three types of union:

1 Those based on trade or craft skills. Their membership is associated with the use of particular skills irrespective of the industry or company in which they are practised. The Boilermakers Society, the members of which are found in many different metal-based industries, is an example.
2 Unions based on industries, although in most cases more than one union will be represented in an industry. Examples are in the

footwear, textile and engineering industries. Some unions are based not only on an industry but on a single employer. The principal examples are in the nationalised industries—mining, steel, railways and others. Examples of company unions in the private sector are rare in Britain.

3 General workers' unions, principally the Transport and General Workers, and the General and Municipal Workers.

Today these distinctions have become blurred. For instance, a category which has shown much growth in recent years is made up of unions representing clerical, technical and managerial employees in industry. These are neither craft nor general unions, but have elements of both in their membership.

Of the present total of about 400 unions over 90 are affiliated to the TUC. There has been a marked reduction in the number of unions since 1971 when there were 525. However this decrease in the number of unions has been accompanied by a corresponding increase in their average size. The ten largest unions have over two-thirds of TUC membership and the present total membership for all unions is more than 10 million.

THE TRADES UNION CONGRESS
The Trades Union Congress is a national body which represents the general interest of the movement at that level, and promotes specific policies in the political arena in support of its aims. For example, much of the recent legislation on employment began as TUC policy

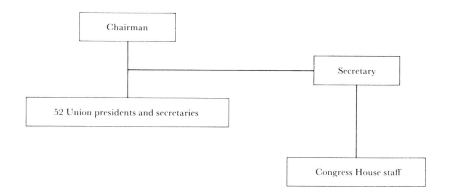

Figure 24    TUC structure

and was subsequently adopted by government and Parliament.

Like most individual unions, the TUC has a headquarters staff, but in essence it is a forum for its member unions. Its governing body is a General Council of 50 members, representing nineteen trade groups. This arrangement will soon change to improve the representative nature of the council—size will be the deciding criterion for council membership. The powers of the council are limited to the pursuit of policies adopted at a full congress of all member unions and are only advisory. The power of the trade union movement rests with its members.

UNION STRUCTURE

There are no firm rules governing the constitution of a trade union. Internal organisations and rules vary greatly. A typical organisation structure of a large union is shown in Fig 25.

The president and secretary of a large union may be public figures

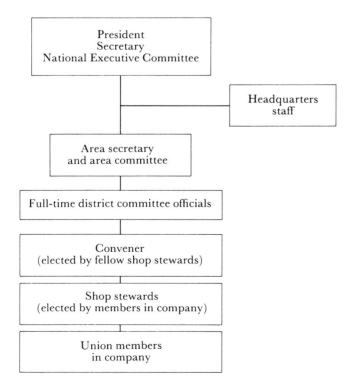

Figure 25    A typical union structure

but they are still representatives of the union membership. As with most democratic institutions, union policy is a mixture of what the lay membership at large press for and what the full-time leadership may advise. As you may have read in the papers union members can, and often do, act independently of union leadership.

You can see from Fig 25 that unions have full-time officials and staff. However, the most important officials in the organisation are the *shop stewards* who represent and lead union members on the shop-floor.

### The shop steward

The job of the trade union in any company is to represent the employees' interests. The shop steward is someone who is both on the company payroll and a union member. As the title implies, he or she is elected by other employees to represent their 'shop' or group of workers on union matters. In a large company there will be many shop stewards and they will themselves elect a representative—the *Convener*.

Shop stewards are not paid for this task and must continue to earn their living like any other employee. However, their special role is generally recognised by management and since 1978 a code of practice has empowered union officials to have 'reasonable time off' for union matters.

Shop stewards represent individual employees when an issue or personal problem has been through the normal company grievance procedure (via the person's supervisor or manager) and still remains unresolved. Companies usually establish with the unions a standard procedure for dealing with such grievances.

The agreement will deal with representation within the company, taking the problem to a higher level at each stage. Most human problems, however, are dealt with readily between individuals and the company without antagonism.

### Full-time union officials

Full-time union officials are available to support the shop steward, especially when matters of principle need to be negotiated with management. Such cases will include discussions on pay and con-ditions, the introduction of new working practices (including new machinery), increases or reductions to the work-force, and other issues affecting the employees as a whole. Full-time officials will be expert negotiators, able to put their members' case to management.

However, they do not have the power to commit union members, who should decide for themselves if they want to accept the solutions put forward.

NEGOTIATION

Negotiation is the process of resolving differences between unions and management. Pay and conditions of service are the most common areas for negotiation, but in recent years job protection and redundancy terms have become increasingly important topics.

It would be wrong to leave the subject of negotiation and the unions without mentioning three additional points. First, there is strong evidence that disputes which appear so often to be about pay are, on many occasions, really about something less tangible. The feeling that an industry is running down and the workers are powerless to do anything about it or poor communication over a period of time between managers and managed are good examples. Secondly, the smaller the unit the less prone it is to dispute. This says something about the role of management and the fact that well-managed organisations tend to have good employee relations. Thirdly, the industries with a bad record in this area are often those which are either in decline or which are going through a period of massive change (eg shipbuilding, coal and steel production).

In many industries a national policy is negotiated between unions and representatives of the employers. For example, the Amalgamated Engineering Union and Engineering Employers Federation will agree a policy for the engineering industry. Agreements reached at national level are not binding on individual companies and their employees, but they provide a guide and a 'floor'. Local negotiations will often result in levels of pay or conditions of employment (holidays, hours of work etc) above the minimum levels negotiated nationally.

UNION RECOGNITION

Union recognition is, like the unions' position in law, the subject of much debate. The laws affecting these matters change regularly, and as this book is written, another change is in the wind. The following situation was correct in the summer of 1983.

Although any employee is free to join a trade union, a company is not bound to recognise a union or enter into negotiation with it unless it has sufficient membership within the company. Where a union has gained recognition in a company, agreement reached between union and company may restrict employees' union membership to that recognised union (or unions). In some establishments the agreement may stipulate union membership as a condition of employment.

Care must be taken to distinguish between two types of agreement which are frequently muddled: a *post-entry closed shop* requires all employees to become members of the union (or one of several unions) recognised by the company; a *pre-entry closed shop* requires prospective employees to be members of a recognised union before employment can be offered. The difference is subtle but important.

It is not uncommon for several unions to be represented in a company or in one of its establishments. For example, in an engineering works, the skilled production employees, the electricians, semi-skilled employees and the clerical staff might each be represented by a specialised union. In addition the drawing office staff might be in the technical section of the AUEW (TASS), whilst supervisors and junior management could be members of a staff union such as ASTMS. It is less common, though not unknown, to find middle and senior managers in union membership.

Generally the importance attached to union membership increases with the size of the company. In a large firm the individual's contact with senior management (as representatives of his or her employer) is often remote, and managers themselves are more obviously employees, like those they manage.

## People and Change

MOTIVATION

In the past most people were driven to work by the stark choice between working and starving. Faced with this choice there was little option but to accept whatever terms of employment were offered. Pressure from unions, successive reforms in employment legislation and a gradual change in the attitude of society, together with a massive expansion in industrial output in this century, have given a degree of opportunity, improved dignity and better conditions to virtually everyone.

Granted that a shortage of work does not now mean starvation, the challenge to managers (bearing in mind the sickness absence figures given at the beginning of the chapter) is to persuade people to work—and to work well. How, for example, do you persuade construction workers to build houses in the rain?

In this environment new methods of motivation have had to be developed. The crude alternative to the 'stick' of unemployment is often thought of as the 'carrot' of more pay. In reality there are other more subtle motivators, many of which stem from a good leadership—a topic which will be covered in the next chapter.

In the present situation of high unemployment, care must be taken to ensure that the old ways do not return. Already there are some worries; the tax and welfare structure of our society has tended to reduce the incentive for some lower-paid workers. The 'poverty trap' means that the modest wages paid for routine tasks can attract tax and also remove eligibility for benefits; in these circumstances you may be better off on the dole than having a job. The present standard of living enjoyed in this country has satisfied the more basic material needs, so that more money no longer acts as a sufficiently strong carrot.

Motivation is as much a social problem as an industrial one but it is faced daily by every manager.

EMPLOYMENT LEVELS AND LEISURE

The establishment of a high standard of living for most people in the UK, and the rest of the Western world, means that wage costs are high. This makes our products and services more expensive than those of developing countries, which can usually take advantage of very low labour costs. This is one of the factors that has contributed to Britain's lack of competitiveness and in turn this has led to a rundown of industry with consequently high unemployment. The textile industry is a good example of this.

The answer to high labour costs must be to use advanced technology, both in terms of designing the product and producing it. There are also opportunities for specialist products and again the textile industry provides examples of companies succeeding against the general trend.

The effect of new technology is to reduce the number of people required in the manufacturing area and there is little doubt that further advances mean a smaller proportion of the work-force will be employed in manufacturing industry. This might not be quite so true for managers in industry and the complexities of this are discussed in greater depth in Chapter 8.

PARTICIPATION

Much has been heard in recent years about 'participation' in industry and it has been suggested that this aspect of work should become part of the law. The basic issues of participation—that is 'by whom?' and 'for what purpose?'—need to be clarified before much progress can be made. One view of participation stems from the belief that the work-force should have a say in the overall direction of their company, through representation on the board of directors. Another is that this type of participation is meaningless to individual workers and that participation only becomes relevant when people are involved with decisions concerning their immediate work situation. If so should such representatives be the nominees of the trade unions or be chosen by all the workers irrespective of union membership?

If the old stick-and-carrot method looks increasingly dated, then other ideas suffer from a conceptual complexity. 'Participation' (as practised in the John Lewis partnership) and 'self management' techniques seem to offer attractive solutions. However, experience suggests they need to be introduced early in the life of the company and they strike at the heart of the hierarchical pyramid structure of existing organisations. Can such ideas be made to work? Perhaps legislation is the answer after all? If not, the question still has to be faced as to how participation can and should be achieved.

# 7

# MANAGEMENT

### The Manager

We often hear people speak about 'workers and managers' as if to suggest that managers do not work. This is not true! Managers are as much workers and employees as anyone else in the company. The great difference between managers and those who are managed is that the former will have a supervisory role that often removes them from the shop-floor. How this happens, and what the manager does, is the subject of this chapter.

The whole subject of management is both complex and controversial. In recent times management science has been one of the fastest growing new disciplines. The USA has given an important lead in the academic study of management techniques and institutions such as the Harvard Business School enjoy international renown. In practice, however, the best of British management is equally highly regarded. Many overseas students come to Britain for management experience and formal management training in our universities, schools, technical colleges and specialist training centres. There has been a steady increase in the export of expertise through consultancy assignments.

This is a surprising state of affairs at a time when it is as popular to lay the blame for poor economic performance on 'management' as much as on the trade unions. It is the very problems which have led to our poor performance which have enabled British management to develop advanced methods and techniques. Where other nations may have been able to overcome problems with massive capital investment we have been forced to evolve sophisticated management systems. The early lead given to the trade union movement by the British people has led to an intricate web of industrial relations calling for far greater skill than the modern, clearly defined and customer-orientated systems such as were introduced into West Germany thirty years ago.

Support for this view is provided in the fact that whilst West Germany has only 17 trade unions, in Britain there are over 400.

DEFINITION

What is a manager? What does he or she do? No single definition of *management* or *manager* exists that is acceptable throughout the business community. Business-school professors, practising industrialists and so-called 'management scientists' all contribute to an ever increasing number of books and opinions. The quickest and clearest explanation of what managers are derives from observation of what they *do*.

Put very simply a manager is responsible for more work than can be done by one individual.

Therefore the distinguishing factor is that people work for managers and it is to these people (their staff) that managers must delegate the many tasks that fall within their area of responsibility.

In consequence the manager may well be responsible as a subordinate to some higher authority, whilst those under him or her may be managers in their own right.

This loose results-orientated definition implies a great many conditions which often don't exist, as we shall see.

Managers are both organisers and administrators, but above all they are leaders. The idea of 'leadership' is sometimes unfashionable but all it means is the process of bringing about the achievement of a task through people.

## Management Structures

MANAGERS AND THE ORGANISATION

Any group of people with a task to do—win a football match, build a house, run a school or whatever—will form themselves into a team. Someone will become the leader; the leader doesn't have to be nominated, one will always emerge. If a leader is chosen, then he or she must have the ability to make the others follow.

If the team is a small one, the leader will be able to influence all the members personally and will be able to make most of the necessary decisions. If the team is large and the task complex the leader will have to divide the team into manageable sections. Each section will have one part of the task to perform and will need its own leader. Some degree of organisation will be required since this will help everyone to understand the way that the team is working, and whom to ask when there are problems.

Charts showing organisational structure are usually drawn in the shape of a pyramid—that is to say with a small number of people at the top and large numbers at the bottom. This reflects the fact that work is assessed according to its difficulty and the amount of responsibility it carries. Only a few people can realistically be charged with policy and decision-making, and this is the responsibility of senior management.

Within the organisation there are leaders—or managers—at many levels. They hold positions of importance in the team, but if the team is to work well everyone must play a full part. A brilliant chief executive cannot get results without the co-operation of the workforce, nor can all the goodwill in the world compensate for inadequate management. Thus the members of all organisations are interdependent and this needs to be recognised by everyone—if the operation is to be pleasant to work in and successful.

THE MANAGER'S AUTHORITY

An essential part of this organisational framework is that the manager is held responsible for the activities and results of all subordinates. If he or she is to discharge this responsibility and be held accountable for results, then the manager must have some say in:

1 Recruitment—or at the very least vetoing the appointment of subordinates.
2 Deciding who does what in the department.

3 Levels of pay and promotion.
4 The training and development of staff.

If managers are not involved in the recruitment process it is hardly their fault if some members of the department turn out to be incompetent. If someone else decides the priorities, allocates the workload or influences who does which tasks, then failure to achieve results will not be the manager's fault. If the effect of another department controlling pay scales results in the worst and the best workers being rewarded equally, then the manager's authority is undermined. If performance could be improved by training, or is suffering from lack of it, then the manager responsible for that performance must have some say in what training and other resources should be allocated. Deciding how much training should be undertaken is a typical managerial task.

Above all it is the manager's primary task to lead staff and to create the conditions whereby they can successfully (and happily) fulfil the tasks which the company pays them to perform. Consequently the kind of life people lead at work is very largely determined by the kind of person they work for.

Managers are held responsible for more work than they can do themselves. Therefore to be effective they must control the payment and selection of their staff, together with the flow of work and the allocation of training. If these matters are not within their authority, then, in all fairness, they cannot be held accountable for the results. People who do not have these essential elements of control may still be called managers but they are not managers in the true sense.

It can be argued that there are not enough real managers in industry. Perhaps many of our industrial relations problems stem from limitations in the authority delegated to 'managers' that prevent them from doing their job and even allow them (with some justification) to avoid taking responsibility for failure.

Of course the definition of management we have used here is rather simplistic. The manager's authority covers a multitude of tasks (eg buying limits, financial control, planning for the future etc) and the job is a great deal more flexible, wide-ranging and complex than has been indicated. Often internal constraints will prevent the manager from doing exactly what he or she believes is necessary. So some degree of frustration is part of the manager's lot.

However, at the centre of it all lies the responsibility of management to those it leads.

ORGANISATION PATTERNS

Given that the manager has the right authority to do the job, the way that subordinates are organised is very important. Most businesses try to present the company structure in simple diagrammatic form. This *organisation chart* is an important document because one of the hallmarks of efficiency is a clear understanding of who does what. It is useful for the employees too, because it shows their position in the team.

Simple diagrams, however, have their limitations. Look at the example of a sales team in Fig 26.

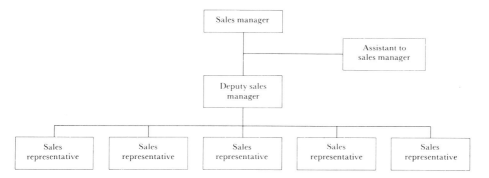

Figure 26

The sales manager has an assistant and a deputy and it all looks very simple. But is it? Can you answer the following questions?

1 Who is the leader of the team of sales representatives?
2 Who is accountable for the results of the team?
3 From whom are decisions obtained?
4 Do decisions on different topics come from different people?
5 How many real managerial jobs are there?

Now look at Fig 27. This organisation chart represents a more accurate picture of what is really happening (or what is supposed to happen). The structure is simple and all the questions asked above are answered.

Organisation diagrams only show the basic and supposedly official relationship between manager and staff. There is also an intricate network of unofficial communication and control through-

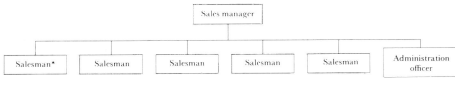

Figure 27                     *Acts as deputy in the absence of the sales manager

out any organisation (including, for example, a school). People with no real seniority seem to enjoy inexplicable influence; people supposedly in charge are disregarded without sanction, and certain people's advice is always sought on particular types of problems.

Thus it is fairly obvious that organisation charts have their weaknesses. However, their strength is that they do show, in a very clear and simple way, who is in charge.

## How Management Works

THE DAILY ROUND
In this book we have talked about the tasks of different departments in a company. The manager's task within all this is to translate the theory into practice. The problem can be divided into three parts:

1 *Understanding what has to be done.* This means the manager must know the technical aspects of his or her department and, by implication, ought to hold a formal qualification.
2 *Deciding how to do it.* This will entail making a plan. Many factors will be involved including time, the personalities and skills of the members of the team, the resources available to help and some ability to anticipate difficulties.
3 *Making sure that the team carries out the plan.* This part of the job requires supervisory skills and personal qualities, such as the ability to communicate and determination.

In order to achieve results the manager will need resources. Planning requires quiet, space to lay out papers and access to all the information that may be needed. Communicating ideas may call for typing facilities or a conference room; a telephone is essential. The daily routine of the manager will be made up of a series of quite simple activities, but there will probably be more variety in it than in the work of other members of the company.

Consider how the sales manager in Fig 26 might start to arrange a conference to brief the sales force on the introduction of a new product.

The date must be fixed. If senior members of the company are to be present diaries need to be checked—perhaps by phone, but more likely a visit to the various offices. When are all the members of the sales team free? Are any of them going abroad or taking a holiday? There will be records to show events like this, but a phone call to each will be sensible to confirm that no new plans are being made. Finding a large room that is free on the right day will take another phone call.

At any stage a major problem might mean that the whole process has to begin again. It could take several days of sporadic effort because the right people are not always in their offices at the right time and may have to be rung back. In the meantime other tasks will continue.

SPAN OF CONTROL

There are limits to the number of people that one person can control properly. If the relationship between manager and staff is to be effective, the number involved is going to be quite small. In fact the accepted optimum number is eight, though arguments can be made to support a figure as large as fifteen. Some managers may claim to control a very large number of subordinates (eg the manager of a supermarket who may have fifty or more people on site). In reality, the only way in which one can control more than a handful of people is by delegating to another level of managers.

This brings us back to the concept of the pyramid discussed earlier. It also poses the question for society as to how to find and train a sufficient number of managers. Is the job attractive enough and do the various national institutions (especially education) assist in the process of developing those with the right qualities?

DELEGATION

The work of a business organisation can be divided by function (eg marketing, production, finance etc) and by level. At the top of any organisation there is a 'chief executive' (or managing director) who operates by making the head of each department accountable for everything relating to that department. Further delegation of responsibility takes place as authority for lesser decisions is handed down. The pyramid again! However, remember the 'MD' is still responsible for the entire operation.

Just as responsibility for different levels of the business is handed down to the next tier of management, the individual manager will, in turn, pass on tasks to his or her staff. This will give subordinates a measure of responsibility but will not, as we have seen, make them managers as such.

Delegating properly is a difficult skill. Some managers delegate too much and lose control whilst others find an understandable tendency towards self-aggrandisement prevents them from delegating fully.

DECISION-MAKING
Decision-making is the manager's prime task. It is a process which can be broken down into the following activities:

1 Defining what is to be done.
2 Assembling the facts and the opinions of other people.
3 Considering the options.
4 Deciding on the right course of action.
5 Communicating the decision to those who will be influenced by it.

In the workplace decisions have to be made at two levels—strategic and tactical. The board of directors must decide the former (often known as policy) whilst the latter normally falls to the managers. They must take many small decisions daily, both to keep the business functioning and to put policy into effect. For example, only the board can take a major decision such as changing the location of the factory. The managers then have to make the move take place—to the right location, at the right time, with the minimum of disruption and without too much personal upset for employees.

Thus deciding what to do is frequently difficult. The temptation is to identify the symptoms of a problem and to attempt to cure them, whilst ignoring the real issue; the parallel is a doctor who, when faced with a case of smallpox, prescribes ointment in an attempt to remove the spots!

In assembling the facts, the manager must call upon his or her own knowledge, experience and training as much as upon the information available. It is unlikely that an engineering problem could be solved by anyone untrained in engineering, however carefully they were briefed.

Most problems can be solved in a number of ways, any one of which would be satisfactory. It is important for the decision-maker to recognise this and to accept that, when all the facts have been assembled, some subjective judgement is necessary.

It may be argued that the communication of decisions is not part of the decision-making process. It is included here because, if people are not told what decisions have been reached (and very often why they have been reached), there can be no action and the decision might just as well have remained untaken.

Many decisions may seem too trivial to warrant such complex handling. They will be reached almost instinctively without detailed analysis. The good manager will recognise those problems which are important and, in doing so, must acknowledge that their solution may take time. In his book *Up the Organisation* Robert Townsend says:

> There are two kinds of decisions; those that are expensive to change and those that are not.
>
> A decision to build the Edsel or Mustang (or locate your new factory in Orlando or Yakima) shouldn't be made hastily; nor without plenty of inputs from operating people and specialists.
>
> But the common-or-garden-variety decision—like when to have the cafeteria open for lunch or what brand of pencil to buy—should be made fast. No point in taking three weeks to make a decision that can be made in three seconds—and corrected inexpensively later if wrong. The whole organization may be out of business while you oscillate between baby-blue or buffalo-brown coffee cups.

The decision-making process presupposes that decision-makers have the strength of character to make up their own minds and to stand by decisions even when they may be unpopular.

One of the key tests for an organisation is not only whether its people can make decisions but, above all, whether they can put them into effect. Decisions taken at board level are worthless unless the management are capable of turning them into action and implementing them daily at all locations.

## Computers and Management

It is fashionable to think of the computer as the solution to all our problems. In previous chapters we have considered how computerisation will affect our lives by its application to an ever widening range of activities. In the context of management the computer must be seen as an aid or tool which can assist but not replace the human leader.

In the course of business a great deal of information is assembled. Much of it relates to quantity. Quantities of stock held, purchase price of items, the current value of each and their whereabouts are simple examples. All this information can be simply referred to as *data*. The generation, recording, updating and extraction of data is known as *data processing*. This is not a new activity; however, its handling by machines is.

Towards the end of the 1950s, electronic machines were introduced to assist in data processing and there has been a steady advance in the sophistication of machinery which continues apace.

Data processing has always been an expensive activity. Before computers arrived, the high cost of clerical staff meant that only essential records were kept and regularly updated. Electronic data processing can be an expensive activity, but it does allow more data to be handled for a given cost than the previous (manual) systems. The capacity of modern machines enables companies to have access to a level of detailed information which was unheard of a few years ago. The result is that business decisions can now be based on the fullest and most up-to-date information. Thus the element of risk and, to some extent, the degree of commercial judgement involved in decision-making has been reduced. Nonetheless commercial managers are still in the risk business.

COMPUTER FUNCTIONS

When asked what is the use of a computer many people reply that it enables things to be done more quickly; they sometimes add the words 'and accurately'. The computer is at its most useful when its twin characteristics of speed and accuracy are employed. Speed can also imply the quantity of data which can be assembled, and used, since there is invariably a finite limit to the time that can be spent on any given task.

The contribution of the computer to management can be considered under six headings, as follows.

*Speeding throughput*

With the aid of a computer the normal time for the completion of work may be reduced. For example, customers' monthly accounts can be made available within hours—instead of days—of the month end, with the possibility of a consequent improvement in cash flow.

*Coping with volume*
When companies grow the volume of work to be handled often becomes unmanageable for the existing staff. More people may not be the best answer because of difficulty in obtaining the right kind, or because the extra work does not justify the additional overhead cost. In these circumstances the computer can be used to cut down the amount of processing handled manually.

*Smoothing peaks*
Most companies are troubled at some time or other by an uneven flow of work. During slack periods staff may be under-employed, whilst at times of pressure delays may occur in the completion of work. Both situations can lead to staff discontent. A computer removes the problem of peaks and troughs by absorbing smoothly the impact of differing work patterns.

*Easier access to information*
There are many situations where immediate access to recorded data of all kinds is desirable, yet not possible through conventional methods of filing and updating. In functions such as credit control, buying and stock-recording, the collation of data is often both complex and time-consuming. Problems may arise as a result of the removal of records by others needing information; or it may be found necessary to produce multiple copies of records, with the problem of keeping them all up to date. The manual control of centralised records can be an expensive operation. It may also lead to staff frustration and disharmony. Computer technology now offers even quite small enterprises a way of maintaining centralised records which are up to date and immediately accessible.

*Increasing management knowledge*
Could management find the answers to questions such as these if it needed to?

How do sales compare with the forecast, by unit and by value?

How do they compare when analysed by product group and by individual product?

Have we such figures for each month and totalled year-to-date, to compare with last year's performance?

Can we split this sales data to compare the performance of sales areas, both home and export?

Which products are returning a margin of profit that has become inadequate?

The answers to all these questions are probably obtainable from existing data within the company. However, the huge clerical effort which finding them would entail would not only be costly, but might produce results too late to be of help. The computer is ideal for the job. It can analyse recorded data quickly and accurately and provide management with vital information (in a variety of different forms) that is absolutely up to date.

*Highlighting irregularities*
In a well-ordered business most activities run smoothly and management need to be told only about irregularities. Speed is vital especially if accounts become overdue or if low or high stock levels develop. By means of a computer such problems are quickly highlighted. By 'reporting an exception', a computer can automatically inform management about problems as they actually develop, enabling early corrective action to be taken.

## The Manager's Attributes

The ability to make firm decisions and to use management aids, like the computer, are only two of the many attributes required of a manager. Others can be seen to stem from the demands of the decision-making process: experience and training, an analytical mind and the ability to carry conviction in putting forward plans.

This means communicating, which is a two-way activity. It involves listening and talking, and knowing when to do which. The manager who listens too much will never reach a decision. One who listens too little won't know what is going on or what people are thinking. Communication through the written word is almost as important.

It would be possible to list many other attributes which are essential or desirable in a manager. Many can be summed up in the one word 'leadership'.

Different qualities will be required and in different measure for each managerial appointment, and companies frequently face a dilemma in deciding which attributes should be pre-eminent. This is particularly true in the field of engineering. Frequently promotion is given to the most able engineer, without regard to the personal qualities that will be required for the role of leader.

Among all these many attributes managers must also have the ability to 'contribute'; to provide from within themselves some element of drive. They must generate the energy to press forward their own part in the overall enterprise. They must set standards of excellence and these can only be derived from their own personal values.

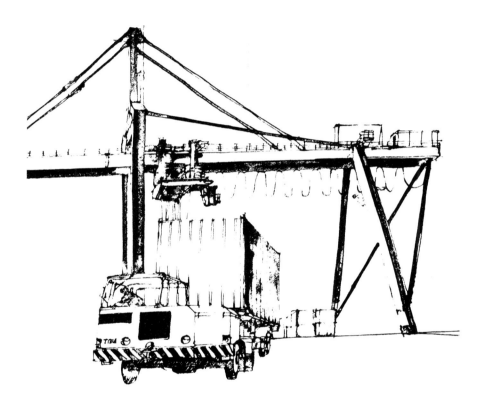

# 8
# SMALL BUSINESSES

So far in this book we have looked at business organisations which are large enough to need a company structure with separate departments—marketing, finance, etc. However the majority of business organisations are small—often comprising less than twenty people. Certain pressures are increasing this trend:

1  Relatively speaking employing people is expensive.
2  Large companies (especially in manufacturing) are not necessarily large employers. Rupert Murdoch can now produce The Times using 450 people instead of 6000.
3  Technological improvements (robots etc) will reinforce the trend away from using people to using machinery.
4  Small businesses are flexible and are good at producing new ideas.

In terms of employment small businesses have an important role. The Small Business Research Trust reports:

> Our best assessment is that unemployment in the UK would be very much higher, perhaps 25 per cent or more higher, if it were not for the new employment in small businesses created during the past six years . . . . . . . . . . . probably 1.1 million jobs are due to small business since 1980.

As you read this chapter you may notice there is no reference to the various departments—sales, finance etc. In your small company (be it your own or someone else's) these divisions will be represented—by you!

It is easier to come to terms with the integration and dynamism of the separate 'functions' if you work in or study a small business. After all every big business started as a small business at one time.

## Why Start a Small Business?

The majority of teenagers at school and college hope, eventually, to get a job working for someone else. Very few ever think about starting their own small business. This is because we live in an 'employee culture' where self-employment is rarely considered. However, things are changing. The rapid rise in unemployment among seventeen to twenty–five year olds has prompted many young people to actively consider working for themselves, some to escape unemployment, others to pursue an idea or to secure their independence.

WHAT ARE THE ATTRACTIONS?

Being your own boss comes top of the list. The satisfaction of being responsible for your own success; not being told what to do; making your own decisions and receiving all the rewards, are some of the attractions. The great variety of activities involved and the satisfaction of solving all kinds of problems as well as dealing with many different people are often quoted as attractive aspects of 'going it alone'. The challenge and opportunities encountered are hard to find in more conventional employment roles. It really is 'putting your money where your mouth is'. Of course it is hard work and there is some risk attached to starting and running your own venture.

In principle, there is no difference between setting up a conventional business (as a sole trader, partnership, co-operative or limited company (see Chapters 1 and 3) and running some venture in the voluntary sector (community work, charity work etc). They both need the same ingredients and they both need to go through similar stages. They both need 'managing'. All are examples of ventures set up to respond to identified local 'needs'

## The ingredients for success

IDEA

To start with you need a *business idea*. It need not be new but it should be one that has a *market,* since an idea without a market is useless.

Virtually everyone has had an idea for a business at one time or another. If you put your mind to it you could probably brainstorm a few dozen ideas based on your skills, hobbies, interests or contacts. Of course the idea must be valid, that is, it should be safe, legal, financially viable and attractive to potential customers.

RESOURCES

Ideas are necessary but they are not sufficient on their own, you also need *resources* to get your idea off the ground. The physical, financial and human resources you need will be unique to your idea. You might need somewhere to work in, somewhere to sell from, transport, stock, equipment, materials, special skills and cash. The amount of cash you need for these start up requirements can be reduced by buying cheaply or secondhand, borrowing or hiring, delaying purchase, doing it in a different way or getting credit. (See Sources of Help page 133).

ABILITIES

However, these resources need to have *skills and abilities* applied to them in order to turn the original idea into reality. There are three kinds of skills needed to set up and run a business:
1  Technical Skills—those skills needed for directly producing your product or rendering your service.
2  Managerial Skills—those skills which focus on forward planning, administration and control.
3  Entrepreneurial Skills—those skills which bring everything together into a successful working whole—leading, selling, negotiating, decision making, idea generation, flexibility, perseverence and successful risk taking.

MOTIVATION

Having an idea and obtaining the necessary resources and skills are all important ingredients for successfully getting your venture off the ground, but nothing will happen without the appropriate *motivation and determination*. You must have the will to succeed. Motivation provides the energy for making things happen and unless you have that energy, together with persistence and optimism, things will fizzle out. Setting up and running a business is an emotionally turbulent period. You will have high and low points, during which friends, family and colleagues can be a great help.

*The need for a plan*

Having a bright idea plus the motivation and capability to see it through is not enough, even supposing you have access to sufficient resources. Your method of getting from an 'idea' to a 'business' needs to be planned in detail. Exactly how will you operate? What precisely is your marketing plan? What are your sales forecasts and are they realistic? Will you make a profit? What is your cash flow going to be like? What about Value Added Tax, Income Tax, National Insurance, planning permission etc? All these questions and more need to be tackled and answered. You need to develop a *business plan*. This is a useful exercise because it helps you think through the logistics and connections in detail. There are agencies which will give you free help in developing your business plan. Of more importance is the fact that banks will not lend unless they are happy with your plan. Your plan is, after all, a statement of what you intend to achieve and how you will do it. It is a document to work from and refer to and both the bank and yourself need to know how you intend to achieve your aim.

THE FACTORS FOR A SUCCESSFUL ENTERPRISE

You need:

1  A valid idea with a market.
2  The motivation and determination to see it through.
3  The skills and abilities to get it done.
4  The necessary resources.
5  A business plan.

However you need not necessarily have all these factors yourself. You can form a partnership or co-operative; you can buy in specialist skills or sub contract particular tasks; you can borrow money and seek grants; you can get help from outsiders with your plan. These 'success factors' are not static things: Ideas tend to change as more is learned about the market and competition; skills and abilities develop with practice; motivation waxes and wanes; resources are fed into and out of the business erraticly and your plan usually needs updating several times in order to reflect actual experience.

## What are the steps involved?

If you start off with an *idea*, the next stage should be to *validate* it. That is, does it work, is it safe, is it legal, will suffficient people buy it etc? This will involve market research and perhaps production of a prototype. A great deal is learned in this phase, particularly through close study of the competition. Most ideas are adapted in the light of experience.

When you are satisfied that your idea is valid, your next step should be to *develop a business plan*. This will involve lots of information gathering—costs, prices, timings, suppliers, possible customers, government regulations and allowances etc—as well as work on estimates, forecasts and calculations. It can take quite a long time to develop a decent business plan but it generally proves to be worth the effort. You can get help in developing your plan (see Sources of Help page 133).

The contents of typical business plan would be:

1  A summary of the major points (written last of all).
2  A brief outline of the idea.
3  Details of the proposer's skills, abilities, experience etc.
4  Description of the market and competition (including your market research findings).
5  The marketing plan.
6  The operating plan.
7  Start up needs.
8  Forecast profit and loss account.
9  Forecast cash flow.
10  Forecast balance sheet.
11  Any appropriate appendices.


Having developed a business plan and identified what you need in terms of loans, grants and overdraft facilities you are now in a position to approach potential lenders—usually the High Street Banks—in order to *negotiate* for a loan or overdraft. You might also be looking for cheap or free premises (Local Authority), grants from grant givers (Local Authority, Prince's Trust, Manpower Services Commission, Department of Trade and Industry, Development Agencies), partners or backers. In addition some private people may wish to invest in your business.

Given that you are in a position to acquire the resources you need you can now *start up* and begin operations. Typically this period is hectic, confused and exciting, since you are doing many things for the first time and making lots of mistakes. You will be discovering many things that you might have overlooked—stationery, record keeping, price lists, credit control etc. You learn by doing and taking advice. You might start off in a small way and part-time so that you do not committ yourself entirely, thus reducing the risk. You will be learning from all your mistakes and discovering the value of personal contacts. Your motivation and determination will be put to the test. However with time, hard work and a bit of luck your business will grow and things will get a little easier.

In general the steps should be:

The Idea
↓
Validate the Idea
↓
Develop a Business Plan
↓
Negotiate for Support
↓
Acquire what you need
↓
Start Up
↓
Operate
↓
Grow
↓

It is easy to get caught up in the doing and making side of the business at the risk of neglecting the marketing aspects. However unless you meet needs in an appropriate manner there will not be enough demand for your product or service.

## Problems in starting up

Typically there are several reasons that people give for not starting their own business:

1 *No business ideas.* This can be easily remedied with a well organised brain-storming session.
2 *Idea does not work.* Think of a new one.
3 *Cannot afford it.* A good plan and some assistance from, say, a local Enterprise Agency can often make it affordable.
4 *Not knowing where to start.* This is common. There are 'start your own business' courses run by local colleges, polytechnics and some

universities, as well as the help from support agencies.

5 *It is too risky.* Risk is usually in the eye of the beholder. Generally people who develop adequate business plans using support agencies have minimised the risks and stand much less chance of failure.

6 *I am too young/inexperienced.* This may be true, but may also be more of an excuse than a reason (see the case studies).

7 *I am not the right type.* This is really an admission that the person feels that he/she has some areas of weakness that needs to be developed, eg self confidence, selling skills, knowledge of 'business'.

8 *I cannot do anything.* This hardly likely to be true. We all have some thing to offer.

9 *It is too much like hard work.* True but it is generally satisfying and rewarding.

Not everyone is capable of starting up on their own, nor might the business idea be viable. Seeking advice, help and support enables people to move things forward and weeds out unsuitable ideas or people. The supprt structure therefore acts as a safety net for non-starters and as an encouragement to feasible projects.

## Case Study—Sandra

Sandra started on a course of teacher training for art and ceramics when she left school. She left the course after eighteen months ex-plaining that it was not for her and anyway she could not stand kids. She had no job to go to and ńothing much in the way of saleable skills apart from her outgoing personality and pottery/ceramic expertise. She took a long working holiday around the Mediterranean 'to think things over' and while she was there she was impressed by the number of young people like her who made money by making and selling craft items to tourists. 'I can do that' she thought and the makings of a plan began to form in her mind.

When she came home she started making ceramic medallions and broaches to sell at craft fairs and similar events. She learned through trial and error which lines and colours sold best and she listened carefully to people's comments and requests. After a few months she had added leather items, hand-made jewellery and coffee mugs to her range of goods. Things were doing nicely after those first few months—when she often had to do without any 'wages' because all her cash was tied up in stock—and she was now using outworkers to make the leather items and jewellery. She was experiencing problems however because she was too successful and too busy. In fact she needed to think seriously about taking on two part-time staff to service the markets and fairs so that she could be free to set up a craft/fancy goods shop. Sandra really wanted £10,000 to get this off the ground and at only twenty years old felt she needed assistance. She got this through an advisor at the local Enterprise Agency who helped her put a business proposal together and negotiate finance from a local bank, under the Loan Guarantee Scheme.

*Sandra started in a small way building on her hobby and skills. She sought help when she needed it.*

### Case Study—Abdul and Ali

Coming to the end of their YTS scheme, Abdul and Ali were depressed and disappointed. Neither of them had got a job to go to, despite the many application forms and interviews they had been through, not did they want to join the family businesses (both families were grocers). They wanted to do things with their hands but, most of all, they did not want to work for their fathers. They wanted to be independent.

The idea of starting up for themselves in their last year at school came quite early on. The only problem was, what could they do? They had £400 between them, the use of a light delivery van and they would soon have plenty of time. Their actual business idea took shape when they were discussing the finer points of car thefts (of which there were many in their inner-city neighbourhood). They would provide a car security service, etching the registration number onto the windows of cars and fitting alarms. All they needed for the etching was a small hand tool, some stencils and a compressor. They could buy the alarms as and when they got an order. They could borrow the van to carry the gear in. They got the business by knocking on doors and asking but soon found that weekdays, 9 am to 5 pm, was not the best time since most cars were being used at that time for travel to and from work. They therefore called in the evenings and at weekends, when both the cars and decision makers were more likely to be at home. Things were slow at first but the £40 a week they each got from the Enterprise Allowance Scheme helped to tide them over. Gradually they got better with their 'sales pitch' and got more efficient at the job. They now see their venture as a stepping stone to grander things once they have built up more capital.

*Abdul and Ali responded to a local need which they identified. They learned from mistakes and adapted accordingly. They see their current venture as a stepping stone.*

### Case Study—The Bunker and other Ventures

Gary, Debbie, David and Vicky were close friends having all attended the local college of further education. Gary and Debbie were almost engaged and had done the catering course, while David and Vicky had done the Business Studies course and fallen in love. They had all been to the same school and regularly went out in a foursome. They felt they had a very good relationship. Both the catering and the business studies courses had 'start your own business' options and these had really fired them with enthusiasm. The decision on what to do and how to do it involved many long and emotional sessions in the pub but eventualy they reached a decision. They would form a catering co-operative.

They sought the assistance of the Co-operative Development agency and started getting their business plan together. What they had in mind was quite an ambitious and diversified operation—a basement bistro called 'The Bunker'; a mobile eats/refreshment vehicle to service the local industrial estate; a 'haute cuisine' meals on wheels service for private dinner parties and a visiting sandwich/snack order service to the many offices and shops surrounding the Bunker. Due to their limited resources and borrowing ability they planned to start with the sandwiches/snacks and haute cuisine services first, then convert the basement premises (for which they needed £2,000). After that they would buy the refreshment vehicle, when they could afford it. The business demanded long hours and hard work and was very trying on their relationships, however after two years they were starting to show a profit. The cooks had learnt to swallow their pride and produce what people wanted rather than what they thought they needed or should have. In addition to keeping the books the business brains had to turn their hands to washing up, preparing vegetables and serving behind the counter.

*With commitment, hard work and realistic plan, they made their dream turn into reality. They enjoy the variety, challenge and job satisfaction.*

### Case Study—Golden Tans Ltd

While some of their contemporaries were struggling to survive on student grants and some others were on the dole, the proprietors of

Golden Tans Ltd each had a company car and were making a very nice living, despite failing their 'A' levels. At twenty, Clare Anthony and Peter Wood were company directors, making and selling sunbeds. Clare had a bubbly personality and knew her way around electrical wiring diagrams, while Peter had a burning ambition to be successful on his own terms. He had excelled at the practical side of C.D.T. at school but failed the theory side. Now they were both proving that it was what you could *Do* rather than what you *Knew* that mattered.

It all started when Peter was trying to repair his mother's sunbed. He found that it was simply a wooden box, some shiny metal, a few ultra-violet tubes and the odd electrical component though it had cost his mother £400. He phoned around and costed the components and found out that the material cost was only about £100 and he knew he could assemble one in about three hours. At first he thought 'what a rip off', then he thought 'what an opportunity'. This would beat living on the dole. He raised the idea with his friend Clare and they spent many hours looking at the advantages and disadvantages of the project. It was a risk and they would need £8,000 to get started. Peter's father offered to put in £1,000 as a long term loan, Peter and Clare had £1,000 between them, they managed to secure a £500 grant from the Council and £1,000 from the Youth Business Initiative. The third bank that they tried offered to match the £3,500 already raised with a medium term loan and in addition to grant a £1,000 overdraft facility. With the help of someone from the Small Firms Service they secured suitable workshop premises (rent and rate free for the first two years) and negotiated trade credit from their two major suppliers.

When they started, Clare and Peter did everything, making, selling, delivery, administration etc—the first six months were exhausting and they were forced to take on an assembly worker. They were surprised to find that this addition more than doubled their output. Following an examination of how they spent their own time they decided to sub-contract the deliveries and to take on a clerk-typist. They were not surprised when their additional sales effort made possible by this decision first produced a 100 per cent and then a 200 per cent increase in sales. They also appointed regional sales agents throughout the country backed by some professionally produced sales literature. They now have three assembly workers, two clerical staff and four commission only salesmen.

*Clare and Peter saw the opportunity and took it. The market was growing and they did their homework first. They shifted their emphasis from production to marketing.*

## Points from the Case Studies

* ⋆ Identifying and responding to local needs is a key feature of entrepreneurial behaviour.
* ⋆ One venture may simply be a stepping stone to others
* ⋆ Starting your own business needs commitment, hard work and a realistic plan.
* ⋆ It provides variety, challenge and satisfaction.
* ⋆ The ability to recognise (and take) opportunities is important, eg a growing market.
* ⋆ Being able to make or do something is irrelevant, in commercial terms, if there is no market for it.

## Summary

Two hundred years ago 80 per cent of the working population of the UK worked on the land; today only about 3 per cent of the work force are in agriculture. The day of farm workers everywhere is gone. Similarly in the nineteenth and early twentieth century manufacturing industry employed the bulk of the working population. Today the manufactring sector is shrinking in terms of employment, whilst the service sector is booming. The world changes, the economy changes, life changes. Before World War II people worked a fifty hour week for fifty weeks a year for fifty years of their life—125,000 hours. Today the trend is towards a shorter working week, working year and working life; something like 40 hours a week for 40 weeks a year (taking holidays, sickness, leave etc into consideration) for 40 years—64,000 hours. A reduction of roughly 50 per cent!

The chances of a person now finding lifetime employment with a single employer are slim. Similarly the likelihood of remaining in the same type of job is remote. The manager and worker of tomorrow will need to be resourceful, adaptable, flexible, independent and quick to learn. Many people will, at some point in their lives, work for themselves. These qualities will be important for people whether as employees or as employers. It is an advantage for a person working in, say, marketing to understand what also happens in production or finance. 'Educated' or 'economically literate' employees should know how the whole operation fits together and works. It is even more important for managers to have an overall view.

Thus whether you eventually join a commercial organisation as a manager or whether your future work is in a wealth-creating support function, we hope this book will have contributed to your understanding of Industry Today.

## Sources of Help

There are many sources of help and the pattern of provision is changing all the time. Once you make your first moves you may come across other forms of assistance. Here are some of the major forms of support.

*British Franchise Association—for information on taking a franchise as a way of starting your own business. Contact: BFA, 75a Bell Street, Henley on Thames, Oxon RG9 2BD.

*British Overseas Trade Board—advice, information and assistance for exporters. Contact: BOTB, 1 Victoria Street, London SW1H 0ET. Tel 01-215-7877.

BSC. (Industry) Ltd—free, cheap and easy money, training, premises and help for start-ups in steel Closure Areas. Contact British Steel Corporation (Industry) Limited, NLA Tower, 12 Addiscombe Road, Croydon CR9 3JH. Tel 01-868-0366.

Competitions—nationally, such as Livewire (sponsored by Shell) and local schemes, such as Headstart in Business—keep your eyes open since these often have financial incentives and practical advice.

Co-operative Development Agency—encourages and assists the setting up of co-operatives. Contact CDA., 20 Albert Embankment, London SE1. Tel 01-211-4633.

CoSIRA—A small Firms Service for rural areas. Contact CoSIRA, 141 Castle Street, Salisbury, Wiltshire.

Department of Employment—(Small Firms and Tourism Division) —there are about 200 government schemes to support business— many of them for new businesses. Contact Small Firms Division, Dept of Employment, Steel House, Tothill Street, London SW14 4NF. Tel 01-405-8454.

*Department of Trade and Industry— for information on investment incentives, Regional Development Grants and grants for Business Improvement Services. Contact DTI, Ashdown House, 123 Victoria Street, London SW14 6RB. Tel 01-212-7676.

Enterprise Allowance Scheme—£40 a week grant for a year to help new starters. Contact your local Job Centre.

Enterprise Zones—there are twenty-five Enterprise Zones across the country where rate relief, tax relief and easy planning permission exist. Contact the Department of Trade and Industry—address above.

High Street Banks—will talk over your proposal with you at an early stage. They have some useful publications and will lend to viable ideas. Contact your local bank and if one turns you down, go to another.

Loan Guarantee Scheme—a loan scheme for small businesses operated through the High Street Banks and backed by the government. Contact one of the High Street Banks.

Local Authority—these offer a range of assistance from rent and rate free premises to grants, loans and assistance. Contact your Industrial Development Officer at the Town Hall/County Hall.

Local College/Polytechnic—more and more further education establishments are offering 'Start Your Own Business' courses. Contact the Department of Business Studies at your local college or polytechnic.

Local Enterprise Agency—specialist help with new starts and small business. Over 300 agencies currently exist all over the country. Their names vary, so in the first instance contact Business in the Community, 227a City Road, London. Tel 01-253-3716.

Managed Workshops—Contact NCB (Enterprise)Ltd, 14/15 Lower Grosvenor Place, London SW1W 0EX. Tel 01-630-5304.

NCB (Enterprise) Ltd—similar to BSC (Industry) but for Coal Mining Areas. Address as above.

Regional Development Agencies—Wales, Scotland and Northern Ireland have their own Regional Development Agencies charged with encouraging and supporting more new indigenous business.

Small Firms Service—publications, advice and signposting on setting up and running. Contact Freefone 'Enterprise'.

Tourist Boards—the English, Scottish and Welsh Tourist Boards offer grants for tourist related projects.

Young Enterprise—This is a student local activity and, along with other organisations, offers school pupils the opportunity to run their own businesses. Your teacher can obtain details of these. Contact Young Enterprise, Robert Hyde House, 48 Bryanstan Square, London W1H 7LN. Tel 01-723-4070

Youth Business Initiative—run by the Prince's Trust and the Royal Jubilee Trust in many areas oif the country. Provides advice and grants to young unemployed people attempting to set up in business. Contact **YBI**, Royal Jubilee Trust, 8 Buckingham Street, London WC2N 7BU.

Youth Enterprise Scheme—provides advice and financial help to unemployed young people wanting to start a business. Contact Practical Action, Victoria Chambers, 16-20 Sutton Ground, London SW1 2HP. Tel 01-222-3341.

## Recommended Reading

*The Guardian Guide to Running a Small Business*, C. Woodcock (Ed), (Kogan Page) £5.95

*How to Start a Workers Co-operative*, J. Brown, Beechwood College, Elsmere Lane, Leeds 8; 95.

*Working For Yourself: The Daily Telegraph Guide to Self Employment*, (Kogan Page) £4.25

*Self Sufficiency, 16-25:* R. Bourne and J. Gould, (Kogan Page) £7.95

*Small Firms Service Publications*, Nos 1 to 20, from Small Firms Service. Free

High Street Banks. Many free booklets

# GLOSSARY

The following is a list of some of the more common terms used in industry and commerce. For further information refer to the index and, if appropriate, the relevant page.

**Account** A record of transactions grouped by category.

**Accounting** The principles and techniques used to establish, maintain and analyse the activities of a business or other type of organisation, usually in financial terms.

**Accumulated profit** Retained earnings. Balance of profit retained in the business and not paid out in dividends. Increase in owners' equity arising from profit earned but not paid out in dividend.

**ADP** Automatic data processing. The systematic sequence of operations performed on data by automatic means, eg merging, sorting, computing with the object of extracting or revising information.

**Amortisation** The process of writing off or reducing the value of an asset over its useful life. Usually refers to intangible assets.

**Arbitration** A way of settling a problem in which both parties to a dispute ask another person or another body to make a decision for them which they both agree to accept.

**Asset** Something of value owned by the business which has a measurable cost. Generally classified as fixed, current or other assets.

**Auditing** Review of accounting records by an independent public accountant.

**Authorised capital** Share capital or amount of capital of the business as authorised by law and approved by the shareholders.

**Backing store** (of computers) A store of much larger capacity than the working store, but requiring longer access time.

**Bad debt** A customer who fails to pay the amount he or she owes to a business.

**Balance** The net amount remaining in an account. Alternatively, the difference between the debits and credits in a ledger account.

**Balance sheet** An accounting report which shows the assets owned by a business and the way they are financed through liabilities and owners' equity.

**Batch processing** Execution of programs such that each is completed before the next is started or the processing of data in a similar serial fashion.

**Board of directors** A policy-making body, made up of the directors of a company.

**Bookkeeping** Recording of transactions. Posting transactions from journals to ledgers to provide basic data for accounting reports.

**Breakeven point** The point of equality between income and expenditure.

**Budget** A financial and/or quantitive statement of the policy to be pursued during a defined period of time to achieve a given objective.

**Budgeting control** A financial control system which provides continuous comparison between forecast and actual results, allowing early remedial action if necessary, or a review of the objective.

**Buying in** The purchase of part-finished or complete components for inclusion in a company's product.

**Capital investment** Major investment in fixed assets and other assets.

**Cash discount** A reduction in price or a discount allowed to a customer for early payment of an invoice.

**Cash transaction** Transaction in which cash is paid or received.

**CBI** Confederation of British Industry, a body that represents employers, including the nationalised industries. The body has a concern for industrial relations as an important part of its job.

**Closed shop** An arrangement by which all the workers in a factory, company or industry must belong to a trade union.

**Collective agreement** The code of rules and practices, especially on wages and conditions, which workers and employers agree to, covering all the members of the employers' and workers' organisations.

**Commission** A sum of money—normally in the form of a percentage—to be added to a person's remuneration as an incentive to improve performance.

**Computer** Any device capable of automatically accepting data, applying a sequence of processes to the data, and supplying the results of these processes.

**Consortium** An association of businesses or industries for a joint activity.

**Consultant** An expert in a particular field, available for consultation, and paid fees for his or her specialised advice.

**Consultation** An interchange of ideas and opinions between management and other employees prior to a decision being made.

**Contribution** The difference between the proceeds of a sale and the direct costs of manufacturing the item.

**Convener** The chief shop steward in a factory or department of a factory. He or she convenes meetings of shop stewards.

**Cost-benefit analysis** A systematic comparison between the cost of carrying out an operation, service or activity and the value of that operation, service or activity. Both cost and value are quantified if possible, taking into account direct and indirect financial and social costs and benefits.

**Cost effectiveness** Getting value for money.

**Costing** The technique and processes of ascertaining the amount of expenditure, either actual or notional, incurred on or attributable to particular products, processes or services.

**Credit** Money owed to someone else.

**Credit transactions** Transaction which results in a liability or debtor. No cash paid or received until later.

**Creditor** One who lends money or extends credit. Shows on balance sheet as a liability.

**Critical path analysis** A planning, scheduling and control technique which uses an arrow diagram as a model.

**Current assets** Assets which are usually realised in cash or used up in operations during the operating cycle (which is usually one year). Includes cash, debtors, stock, prepaid expenses.

**Current liability** Liability normally due for payment within one year.

**Data** All, or any selection of, the operands and results involved in any operation or set of operations. *Note* 1 The word 'data' although plural in form is commonly used as a collective noun and may therefore be used with a singular verb; 2 The use of the word 'information' to mean 'data' is deprecated. In its ordinary sense the information associated with data is what the data conveys to the person receiving it.

**Data processing** A systematic sequence of operations performed on data, eg merging, sorting, computing, manipulation of files with the object of extracting information or revising it.

**Debentures** Long-term loans.

**Debt** Liability, money due to someone else.

**Demarcation** Definition of jobs arising from an agreement between unions which permits a job to be carried out only by a member of an appropriate union. This can lead to inflexible methods of working.

**Depreciation** The process whereby the cost of a fixed asset is allocated to expense over its working life.

**Digital computer** A computer using numbers (digits) to express the variables and quantities of a problem. This type of computer is normally used for business applications.

**Direct cost** Cost which can be directly attributed to a product, service or unit of production.

**Director** Appointed by the shareholders, directors are responsible to them for the efficient running of the company.

**Disc** A magnetic store in which the magnetic medium is on the surface of a rotatable disc.

**Discounted cash flow** The allocation of a suitable rate of discount to forecasts of additional future outlay and income relating to a project, to take account of their incidence over the life of the project.

**Discretion** The ability to exercise personal judgement within limits set by policy.

**Diversification** Increasing the range of interests, activities or output of an organisation so that problems or losses arising in one sector may be offset by stability or profitability in others, thus minimising harmful effects on the whole organisation.

**Dividend** That part of a company's profit that is paid to shareholders at so much per share.

**End user** The person who uses the product. Manufacturing companies may sell their product to wholesalers or shops who are their customers, but are not the end users.

**Factoring** The buying in of finished goods by a manufacturing company for resale as part of its own range of products.

**Fixed assets** Assets acquired for long-term use in the business and not for resale. For example, land, buildings, plant and equipment.

**Fixed cost** A cost which tends to be unaffected by variations in volume of output, depending mainly on the passage of time.

**Flow chart** A diagrammatic presentation which shows the logical progression of actions and decisions leading to a conclusion.

**Fringe benefits** Items which form part of some agreements between unions and employers in addition to 'wages and conditions'.

**Grievance procedure** The rules and practices laid down within a factory or an industry by which problems, disputes or grievances should be settled.

**Hardware** (of computers) Physical equipment as opposed to the computer program or methods of use. ( See also **Software**)

**Historical costing** The ascertainment of costs after they have been incurred.

**Hygiene factors** A term used in management circles for the basic factors of administration, eg welfare, pay, environment.

**Indirect cost** Expense which cannot be directly attributed to a product, service or unit of production. Overhead.

**Industry Training Boards** Government bodies set up for each industry (eg engineering, hotel and catering) to ensure that the people within that industry are properly trained.

**Interface** A shared boundary, for example the boundary between two sub-systems or two devices.

**Invoice** Bill for goods or services provided.

**Issued capital** Shares actually issued or sold by a company. Shown as part of owners' equity in the balance sheet.

**Job evaluation** A method of determining the relative standing, for pay purposes, of jobs within an organisation, or part of an organisation.

**Lead time** The actual or expected time between the start of an order for work and the completion of it.

**Liability** The claims of creditors or outsiders against the assets of a business. Amounts to be paid to others.

**Line management** The chain of command and control.

**Line manager** A manager who is actually engaged in providing the goods or services of the company, ie production manager as opposed to staff manager.

**Line responsibility** Responsibility for the performance of subordinates.

**Management** A business process involving the continuous planning of operations and the control of resources, in fulfilment of a given aim. Also the collective term for a managerial body.

**Management by objectives** A system of management in which objectives are fixed, thus forming yardsticks against which both a manager and his or her subordinates can measure performance. Responsibilities are defined, and through improved communication the workers have increased participation in the whole operation, so achieving greater effectiveness.

**Margin** The difference between the proceeds of sale and the purchase price of goods.

**Mark-up** The amount added to the cost of purchasing an item to ascertain a sales price.

**Mortgage** A long-term loan normally secured on fixed assets, such as a house or property.

**Negotiation** A formal procedure by which management and unions resolve differences, eg over grievances, wages, terms and conditions of employment. (Any solution reached is essentially a two-sided affair—a bargain—and both sides are therefore responsible for carrying through the bargain.)

**On-line** (of computers) Pertaining to equipment or devices under the control of the central processing unit, or to a user's ability to interact with the computer.

**Organisation and Methods (O&M)** An advisory service for management specifically designed to assist in obtaining maximum efficiency and accuracy in organisation and procedures. The application of work study and other management techniques to administrative procedures and systems within a company.

**Overdraft** A short-term or temporary loan from a bank.

**Overhead** An indirect cost or expense which cannot be conveniently associated with a unit of production.

**Parent** A parent company owns a majority of the voting stock of another company which is known as a **subsidiary**.

**Patent** Legal right to prevent exploitation of an invention or process by someone else.

**Peripheral** (of computers) Any unit of equipment, distinct from the computer's central processor, which provides the system with outside communication.

**Policy** The means whereby an objective is to be achieved.

**Productivity** The relationship between output and resources/effort expended.

**Productivity deals** Production refers to the total amount of goods or services produced, whereas productivity refers to the output of workers generally measured in production per hour. A collective agreement takes place when the employers and unions agree to alter their practices in return for concessions from either side in relation to productivity.

**Profitability** A measure of financial return, eg the ratio of profit made to capital expended.

**Profit and loss account** Often known as the P and L account. A statement of trading and other activities over a given period (usually one year).

**Program** A set of instructions and any other necessary data for controlling a computer run. The spelling has been adopted to distinguish it from other types of programme such as a production programme or a programme of work.

**Public relations (PR)** The deliberate planned and sustained effort to establish and maintain mutual understanding between an organisation and its public.

**Quality control** The maintenance of established standards of materials, size, weight, finish, etc, for goods or services.

**Real time** In step with events being simulated, or at sufficient speed to analyse or control external events happening concurrently.

**Redundancy** The word now being used for the situation in which workers lose their jobs, because there is insufficient work to justify their continued employment, or because their task has been discontinued.

**Resources** A combination of labour, money and material.

**Restrictive practices** Actions taken by workers to protect their jobs in which they may put restrictions on output, speed of working, or who shall do which job, or by employers to protect their prices or selling arrangements.

**Sales discount** Cash discount on sales usually extended for prompt payments.

**Sales expense** Expenses incurred in promoting sales and retaining customers.

**Security** Collateral provided against a loan or liability (alternatively, a financial investment such as a stock or a bond).

**Share** Certificate certifying ownership of shares in a company. A share represents the minimum subscription a member can hold in a company, eg one share of £1 nominal value out of an issued share capital of £1 million.

**Share capital** A part of owners' equity. Refers to money put into a business by the owners.

**Shop steward** An elected member of a group of trade unionists who acts on their behalf.

**Single status/Staff status** Giving both 'blue' and 'white' collar workers the same terms and conditions of employment.

**Software** The collection of programs and routines associated with a computer. (See also **Hardware**)

**Spin-off** A by-product or offshoot.

**Staff association** A body set up by an employer to negotiate on behalf of the employees instead of an independent trade union.

**Staff responsibility** Responsibility for the providing of specialist services.

**Structure** The definition of the various roles within the company, and the interrelationship existing between these roles.

**Subsidiary** A subsidiary company is an entity of which the majority of the voting stock is owned by another company.

**Supervisor** One who oversees the implementation of managerial directives.

**Tender** An offer to carry out work or supply goods at a stated price.

**Terminal** A point at which information can enter or leave a communications network. A device, usually equipped with a keyboard and some kind of display, capable of sending and receiving data over a communication channel.

**Time sharing** A method using a computing system that allows a number of users to execute programs concurrently and to interact with the programs during execution.

**TUC** Trades Union Congress.

**USP** Unique Selling Points. Those features of a product or service which set it aside from similar material.

**Value analysis** An organised way of reducing unnecessary cost without prejudice to quality.

**Variances** The difference between an actual cost and a forecast (budget) cost.

**VDU** Visual Display Unit. A display of data on a television-type device or by light-emitting diodes in a viewing window, etc.

**Word processor** A machine used to facilitate the composition, editing, reproduction etc of text.

**Work study** A management service based on method study and work measurement, used to examine human work in all forms. Improvements to the situation under review result from a systematic investigation of all the relevant resources and factors.

**Works council** A body set up in a place of work with members drawn from all sections of the workplace whose job it is to consider issues which affect the whole works, and which is used by management to canvass the views of employees and to consult them on issues that affect both groups.

# BIBLIOGRAPHY

Local librarians can recommend reading on different aspects of industry. In addition the following books and booklets are suggested for further reading.

GENERAL

*Understanding Organisations*, Charles B. Handy (Penguin)

*Up the Organisation*, Robert Townsend (Coronet)

*Industry and Empire*, E. J. Hobshaw (Pelican)

*The Multinationals*, Christopher Tugendhat (Pelican)

*The Business of Management*, Roger Fack (Pelican)

*Starting Work*, Hilary Adamson and Mazzie Lewis (The Industrial Society)

*The Work Challenge*, John Garnett (The Industrial Society)

*The Teachers' Treasure Chest*, Schoolmaster Publishing Company (Exley Publications)

*The Future of Work*, Charles B. Handy (Basil Blackwell)

MARKETING

*The Fundamentals and Practice of Marketing*, John Wilmhurst (Heinemann)

*Marketing: An Introductory Text* M. J. Baker (Macmillan)

*Case Studies in Marketing*, Charles Dunn (Papermac)

*Retail Business Management*, Gillespie and Hecht (McGraw-Hill)

*How to Advertise*, K. Roman and J. Mass (Kogan Page)

RESEARCH, DEVELOPMENT AND DESIGN

*About Design*, Ken Baynes (Design Council)

*Let's Look at Design*, C. G. Romrley (Frederick Muller)

*Design Education: Problem-solving and Visual Experience*, Peter Green (Batsford)

*Design in General Education*, (Ed) John Harahan (Design Council)

MANUFACTURING

*Manufacturing Processes*, Herbert W. Yankee (Prentice-Hall)

*Manufacturing Technology*, G. Bram and C. Downs (Macmillan)

*Production Engineering Technology*, J. D. Radford and D. B. Richardson (Macmillan)

*Manufacturing Technology*, M. Hazelhurst (English Universities Press)

*Production Decisions*, John Powell, Understanding Business Series (Longman)

FINANCE
*Money—whence it came, where it went*, J. K. Galbraith (Pelican)
*Business accounting 1*, Frank Wood (Longman)
*How the Stock Exchange Works*, Norman Whetnall (Flame Books)

PERSONNEL
*A Textbook of Personnel Management*, George Thomason (IPM)
*The Practice of Personnel Management*, David Barber (IPM)

MANAGEMENT SERVICES
*Work Study*, W. Richardson, Secondary Science Services (Longman)
*Teach Yourself Organisation and Methods*, R. G. Breadmore (English Universities Press)
*Organisation and Methods*, R. G. Anderson, M and E Handbook (Macdonald and Evans)
*Industrial Management Services*, H. Beeley, M and E Handbook (Macdonald and Evans)

STRUCTURE AND SIZE
*Small is Beautiful*, E. Schumacher (Fontana)

MOTIVATION
*The Human Side of Enterprise*, D. McGregor (McGraw-Hill)
*Involvement: From Communication to Participation. Communication In Organisations*, Lyman W. Porter and Karlene H. Roberts (Penguin)
*Industrial Relations and the Trade Union Movement. Trade Unions*, (Ed) W. E. McCarthy (Penguin)
*A History of Trade Unions*, Henry Pelling (Pelican)

INDUSTRY AND SOCIETY
*Why Industry Matters*, Julia Cleverdon and Patrick Wintour (The Industrial Society)
*Facts of Life*, Richard Redden (Macdonald)
*The Economic Facts of Life*, Wilfred Sendall (Ibis Databank International Limited)
*Nationalised Industries*, Graham L. Reid and Kevin Allen (Pelican)
*A Guide to the British Economy*, Peter Donaldson (Pelican)

TECHNOLOGY AND CHANGE
*The New Industrial State*, J. K. Galbraith (Pelican)

# INDEX

# WE SEE OPPORTUNITIES WHERE SOME SEE ONLY RISKS.

3i is the largest source of venture capital in the world.

We're ready to provide finance for your business whether you want £100,000 or £10 million.

Currently we have investments in 4,500 companies totalling £1,600 million.

It's worked for them. It can work for you.

THE CREATIVE USE OF MONEY.

# Students notes

# Student Notes

# Student Notes

# Student Notes

# Student Notes

# Student Notes

# Student Notes

# Student Notes

# Student Notes

# Student Notes

# Student Notes

# UNDERSTANDING INDUSTRY TODAY
## G. M. J. Richardson
### Edited by Antony Wood

Neary 21 million people are involved in industry and commerce in Britain today, but many others have no idea what happens inside business organisations. *Understanding Industry Today* explains this enormous area of our society in a clear and manageable way, by dealing with its component parts: structure, finance, marketing and sales, technology, design and manufacture, people, and management.

This book is derived from a series of booklets designed to support the Understanding Industry course, used by sixth-form colleges, 'A' level classes, F.E. colleges, undergraduates and teachers. It is not an academic text book, but the distilled thoughts of many people who are earning their living at the sharp end of today's industry.

**The Author/Editor**
The original text for this book was written by Gerry Richardson, who as Managing Director of Investors in Industry Consultants Ltd planned and conceived the Understanding Industry (UI) programme. The text has been edited by Antony Wood, Director of UI on secondment from 3i.

Antony Wood is an expert on industrial liaison and his time is largely spent visiting schools and universities to lead discussions on business affairs and careers in industry. Before becoming a consultant, he worked in industry, in production planning, purchasing, recruitment and sales, followed by a period as operations manager for a small high-technology company.

## Understanding Industry

- Is a national organisation with over 25 regional organisers
- Aims to give 16–19 year olds a better understanding of industry and commerce
- Arranges structured courses in school and college timetables. The courses are participative in style
- Invites local managers to volunteer for the programme and explain their specialism
- Is supported by the DTI, DES, industry and commerce